GARDENS FOR ALL SEASONS

GARDENS FOR ALL SEASONS
PUBLIC GARDENS AND ARBORETA OF MARYLAND

by

WAUNETA B. WINE

VANDAMERE PRESS
a division of AB Associates

Published by
Vandamere Press
A division of AB Associates
P.O. Box 5243
Arlington, Virginia
22205

Copyright 1988 by Vandamere Press

ISBN 0-918339-09-X

Library of Congress Cataloging-in-Publication Data

Wine, Wauneta B.
   Gardens for all seasons.

   1. Gardens--Maryland--Guide-books. 2. Arboretums--
Maryland--Guide-books. 3. Maryland--Description and
travel--1981-   --Guide-books. I. Title.
SB466.U65M38 1988   712'.025'752   87-27897
ISBN 0-918339-09-X

Manufactured in the United States of America. This book is set in Basker-
ville Roman. Typography by Chronicle Type & Design, Washington, D.C.

Dedicated to Community Volunteers with Beautiful Visions, Generous Hearts and Dirty Hands

It must be true that man has loved all of the flowers on earth, as well as the trees, the shrubs, the herbs and the grasses that wave before the wind. They have been subjects of poetry, song, and suitable for labor. They are acquired and they are given; they are shared and they are secretively stashed away. Many of the gardens herein exist because of the love and devotion of community volunteers who care for them. This book is dedicated to those tireless supporters.

Garden Flowers

Which is God's favorite flower? none knows,
The lily or the June time rose,
or brightening some secluded spot
The tender, pale forget-me-not
With differing leaf and blooming stem,
no two alike from Spring to Fall,
It must be that He loved them all.

unknown

ACKNOWLEDGEMENTS

I am indebted to many people for assistance with this book. In the beginning, I wrote to the Agricultural Extension Agents in all of the counties of the state in order to begin the collection of names of gardens and/or arboreta. They were very helpful in locating the gardens. That was true even for the agents who, after considerable search, had to tell me that the county had no public gardens.

The curators/owners of the gardens have graciously taken the time to assist me with information and access to the gardens for photographic trips. Without their help I could not be sure that the information which is enclosed is accurate.

The St. Mary's City Commission represented by Karin Stanford has coordinated my trips to St. Mary's City involving meetings with various people to instruct me and introduce me to their gardens. Ms. Stanford greatly aided this project. Henry Miller, Ph. D. of St. Mary's City Commission, provided me with background for the archaeologist's role in garden restoration. Assistance has also been given by the United States Department of Agriculture at Beltsville; from both the Office of Small Grains Collection and the Library. Dr. David Percy of the Accokeek Foundation at the National Colonial Farm granted me audience that verification might be made on the evolution of the seed saving programs. Elizabeth Wardlaw, reviewed the text to check for the inclusions of corrections. Deborah Stephenson, cartographer, assisted in the creation of the trail guides.

To my editor, Pat Berger, and publisher, Art Brown, who have watched and worked with me to make this dream a reality and to my friends Virginia Pausch and Dr. Virginia Pond who proofed the galley copies and who have cheered me on over my educational and professional journey I offer my thanks.

Last, but far from least, is the support of my husband and children. Going to college with your children is an experience that I would wish for anyone. Without my husband it would not have been possible to have a thirty-five year marriage, raise and educate three children and educate ourselves, (I worked and he went to school and he reciprocated the favor.), and he watched with encouragement as I began my professional life and has been my lifeline in the tangled net of computers. Thank you, Jim.

To all who have helped and have not been named I say that you are as numerous as the volunteers who keep the gardens going. Thank you everyone.

Wauneta B. Wine

TABLE OF CONTENTS

LIST OF ILLUSTRATIONS

CHAPTER ONE
Wherefore Gardens?

When the first colonists arrived in the area that was to become Maryland, they had a rich gardening history behind them. They also had seeds in their pockets and snips and clips of plant material with which to begin gardens for their new homes. Most were ill-prepared, however, for the realities of this new land, its heat and humidity, and the new diseases to be found by man, beast, and plant. In all three cases the hearty ones survived.

An imaginary time line could be laid out and the gardens of Maryland plotted upon it. The American Indian Garden at St. Mary's City would undoubtedly begin the time line, as it was present when the colonists arrived in the early 1600s. It is the most rudimentary of all of the gardens, with small mounds of earth scraped up and seeds pressed in. The gardens to immediately follow it would be more sophisticated though still geared to survival. The American Indian Garden and those immediately following it exist today as reconstruction gardens with some of the earliest ones also being in St. Mary's City.

Reconstruction gardens are composites or aggregates of information about the gardens of the time period represented. Information is derived from archaeological sites, plantation records, letters of gardeners to friends and relatives, art work by artists of the period, or court recordings. Often court recordings are the most revealing, such as one detailing the complaint of one landowner against the actions of a neighbor's cow that broke into the plaintiff's garden, doing considerable damage. The listing of the damaged crops reveals the contents of the garden. Once this information is assembled and verified to be historically correct, a garden may be planted.

Visiting the representative gardens of those early days, a guest would learn of the necessity and problems of survival, particularly if the visit was during a dry summer. The colonists had to have energy-efficient gardens, as the gardens received precious little tender loving care. Time and energy spent on watering were out of the question. Productive, utilitarian gardens were not meant to be beautiful. There may well be beauty to be found in them, but these gardens were first of all a part of survival rather than a pleasant luxury of color and beauty.

Plants gathered by early herbalists became the forerunners of the herb gardens tenderly cared for today. These gardens speak of the history of cooking, dyeing, medicine, insect repellant, and superstition. It is interesting to look at a list of herbs and their uses to see how many times people used an herb without much more to go on than an unfounded belief that it would cause a desired effect. English Lavender, *Lavandula angustifolia*, was a favorite of the colonists for a variety of tasks from scenting closets to curing trembling of the limbs. Borage, *Borago officinalis*, was believed to bring happiness.

The few fruit trees to one side of the early sheltered garden were referred to as the "dessert garden." They speak of man's sweet tooth. In time the fruit trees moved out and became orchards with many special varieties.

Next on the time line would be the gardens found in the interior of the state. Most of them are either from plantations that survived through the years, or reconstructions in part or in whole, of farms, estates, or townhouses. Some of these gardens were utilitarian, but others were labors of love and money. Gardening as a devotion requires the owner to have an abundance of all the necessities of life so that he can turn his attention to the tender loving care necessary to cultivate plants for no reason other than the owner's special interest. From the luxury of wealth and the assistance of hired (or owned) gardeners to pluck, train, trim, scythe, pollinate, water, and harvest came the pleasure gardens, croquet lawns, and bowling greens. The crowning touch was the inclusion of the "orangery." Within these precious glass enclosures grew "luxury" fruits for those who could afford them. For the tables of the wealthy paraded a steady stream of peaches, oranges, grapes, and other delectables at a time when the bitter winds of winter blew.

Among the most pampered gardens are the parterre gardens of William Paca (Paca House in Annapolis) and Charles Ridgely (Hampton Mansion in Baltimore). Parterre gardens are formal gardens divided by paths between the beds. In both the Paca and Ridgely gardens, the gardens are also on multi-levels, reached in one case via steps and in the other by means of grass slopes. Both gardens had the space and the means to be developed into pleasure gardens with beds devoted to the flowers, shrubs, and trees that appealed to the owner. While the poorer gardeners had to hope for rain, Paca had a spring and the gardens at Hampton Mansion had the ultimate luxury of wooden irrigation pipes.

Some gardeners like Paca and Ridgely were devoted to their formal gardens. Others were more interested in the form of the plants *per se*. Harvey Ladew of the Ladew Topiary Gardens went to work with shears, imagination, and a crew of help to design a garden of "topiary." The largest topiary garden in the United States created by one individual has been the result. It is known internationally.

If topiary turned plants into animal and structural forms, bonsai was the faithful miniature representation of the full-sized plant world. Half a world away in Japan, gardeners wielded the same kinds of pruning shears, training wires, and imagination to create bonsai and set a mood in miniature plant form. Imitations of boulders were suggested by small rocks; ancient trees twisted and worn by the elements were carefully developed by the use of pruning shears and wire. A living stage was set for a long life of love and tender care that occasionally spanned several generations of the relatively short-lived gardeners. This art came to Maryland at a later date and is seen in the

Japanese Tea Garden in the Mable Walter Arboretum in Hagerstown.

As interest in the plant world became more of a hobby, gardens in Maryland became more varied and at the same time more specific. Gardeners grew only the plants of their interest, such as orchids, bearded iris, or lilies. Some gardens became "single season" gardens, cared for ten months out of the year in anticipation of the pleasure that they presented in the one to two months that they bloom. Thus, there are all azalea or all tulip gardens today.

Genetic engineering was not always known by its 20th century name, but it has been practiced as long as man has noticed that some plants were different from their siblings and selectively saved the seeds from the preferred specimens. Later, horticulturists learned to hand-pollinate plants to create hybrids. Horticultural advances in the 17th, 18th, and 19th centuries involving varietal specimens, hybrids, sports, and production control caused an unintended removal of a wide array of plants from the countryside. Not a deliberate action, this was a gradual erosion caused by several factors. First, appearance of new hybrids on the market removed the older strains of cultivated plants. Second, small farms were turned into massive, single-crop enterprises and many of the hedgerows were removed where conglomerates of wild plants had survived. Third, herbicide for the control of weeds removed the weeds from the fields, and at the same time, drift of that same herbicide removed the wild plants within drift range. Unfortunately many of the plants removed were the sturdy native stock of these same new and sometimes sterile specimens. Soon genetic engineering began to be a source of problems as well as a source for their solution.

By the early 1900s, a few gardeners across

the nation with concerns about this erosion to the original plant gene-pool-material began a new kind of "old" gardening. Gathering the seeds of older and less popular strains and the cuttings of older shrubs and searching for individual specimens of nearly extinct trees, heritage gardeners began seed banks. Seed savers and other plant conservation groups dedicated themselves to holding for possible future needs these more viable, often less susceptible to disease, varieties. The United States Department of Agriculture in Beltsville, Maryland, set up a seed bank, the National Small Grains Collection in 1948. In 1981, the Seed Savers Exchange formally created a Growers' Network in Iowa. From a handful of seed carefully nurtured and harvested in a garden setting, enough grain could evolve in a few seasons to plant a field, thus restoring a stock greatly depleted.

Without intention of collaboration, several Maryland gardens began to save from the past for the future. The National Colonial Farm in Accokeek is one of those gardens devoted to the salvation and increase of many seeds that have been dropped from the commercial world or crowded out of the natural world. Making their beginnings with seeds from the Seed Savers Exchange, the National Small Grains Collection, and their own breeding and genetic selection program, the National Colonial Farm is adding to this heritage. The Carroll County Farm Museum, the Paca House, and the Hampton Mansion gardens all have heritage roses of the 17th, 18th, and 19th centuries. The herb gardens across the state carry forward those useful-to-man plants within their borders.

At the close of the time line are found the gardens of the present. Their purposes vary much as they always have. Man's pleasure in growing things, creating new plants, being out-of-doors, and appreciating the green world are traditional gardening goals. Education has become a new task of the curators of public gardens and is aimed at the young and old, gardener and non-gardener, and urban and suburban resident. Gardens work to be open and available to the handicapped. Ramps, paved paths, and raised beds are included in the modern gardens to assist the wheelchair-bound visitor in seeing the gardens and getting close to plants. Sensory gardens are grown for the visitor to touch, taste, and smell the plants within. New gardens have been created for the pleasure of the public by local government groups and volunteers. Some are memorial gardens while others have multiple purposes; still others are part of a park development.

Gardens and Arboreta

With the end of winter, people want to get out-of-doors. Many head for the nearest park or public garden. The gardens are beautiful to see and enjoy after the long, dim days of winter. They are full of color, and the air is cleaner and warmer. When spring passes, all too often the visitors feel the gardens are past their prime. The true garden devotee knows that this is not the case, except with the single season garden.

This book is designed both photographically and journalistically to stimulate the reader to go visit the gardens in the summer, autumn, and dead of winter as well as spring. We have gardens for all seasons. Not every garden is an all-season garden. Appendix A provides a table outlining the gardens and their qualities as well as their best seasons.

Gardens and arboreta have been grouped together in this book. Technically there is a difference. A garden is a plot of ground where fruits, vegetables, and flowers are grown and an arboretum is a collection of specimen trees, shrubs, and herbs. In reality, the two often overlap. Most arboreta have gardens within their borders. Certainly London Town, Cylburn, Greenway, Washington Temple, and Walter Arboretum all have many gardens within their bounds. Likewise, many of the "gardens" have specimen trees on their premises. The gardens and arboreta in this book represent a broad spectrum of plant display within the state.

Three of the gardens included in this work are commercial. Even so, they have become a part of the community within which they operate, offering classes open to the public and lending their gardens to the community in different ways. Lilypons, the largest, has two devoted groups of repeat visitors, garden enthusiasts and bird watchers who see the gardens secondarily as they follow their first love, waterfowl. The two remaining are herb gardens that serve their communities with guided tours, open gardens, lectures, and classes.

The "public" gardens contained in this book were chosen because of their availability to the public and their interest potential as gardens, regardless of the presence or absence of a resident structure. There is minimal treatment of any such resident structures for the gardens included. There are many fine books that deal with these historic homes, estates, plantations, and other remarkable sites within the state. Gardens that are decorations for historic buildings are not included. A great deal of effort has been made to insure that no public gardens in Maryland have been overlooked; however, it is possible that this has happened. If so, the author extends apologies.

The gardens included in this book were viable at the time of their inclusion. The health of the garden is dependent on the health of those individuals or the financial institution

CREAM SATIN: PLEASURE GARDENS OF WILLIAM PACA
Creamy white petals laid open on forest green leathery leaves, *Magnolia grandiflora*, stud the large tree standing as a cornerstone to the Pleasure Gardens of William Paca.

PARTED IN GREEN: PLEASURE GARDENS OF WILLIAM PACA ▲
The Holly Parterre and the Flower Parterre of the Pleasure Gardens of William Paca were reconstructed from information gleaned by the archaeologists and historians. Holly in both topiary forms and those allowed to grow according to their normal pattern are part of the collection of holly in the Holly Parterre Garden.

LEMON FRILLS: HELEN AVALYNNE TAWES GARDEN ▶
Open for one brief day, the day lilies at Helen Avalynne Tawes Gardens enjoy a sunlit bed bordering a small circular walk. This bed, symbolic of the open spaces of the state with its sunshine and fresh air, has a succession of sun-loving plants.

MINI-FINGER LAKE: Helen Avalynne Tawes Garden ▲
Fed by a tiny stream lying in the Helen Avalynne Tawes Garden, this little pond stands for the many bodies of water across the state. A representative garden captures the settings of the different sections of the state. Water, woodlands, and shore are shared by winged and four-footed visitors as well as the people who join them.

HIDE AWAY: Arboretum of the London Town Publik House ▶
Off the beaten path, a bench in the London Town Arboretum welcomes the tired, the contemplative, or even the lunchtime visitor. Seated in such a glade listening to birdsong, one can easily slip away from the cares of the world for just a little while.

LAVENDER FALLS: Arboretum of the London Town Publik House ▶▶
Japanese Iris bloom at the London Town Arboretum. Rich stands of Japanese Iris send their stalks of blossoms upward from the damp banks of the pond within the glade. Beautiful blossoms with rich tints and shades of lavender are marked with tints of the same color, white, or gold.

COLORFUL LAKE: Sherwood Gardens ▲
A soft breeze ruffles the flowing blossoms as it once ruffled the waves of a small lake where Sherwood Gardens now bloom in such profusion. This single season garden of 80,000 tulips is a must on the calendars of thousands of visitors every spring.

READY FOR THE HOLIDAYS!: City of Baltimore Conservatory ◀
In spite of the weather outside, row upon row of display plants create a tiered effect as poinsettias and Norfolk Island Pine set the stage for the holidays at the City of Baltimore Conservatory. Wintertime is the most attractive time at the conservatory; the air is warm and fragrant and the flowers are beautiful.

SERPENTINE OF GOLD: Cylburn Arboretum ▶
Seen close up, golden coxcomb is just one of the many plants bedded in the All-American Selection Display Garden in Cylburn Arboretum. Displayed in neat rectangular beds, these flowers are the winners of the All-American Selection in previous years. Some selections will be coming on the market in the near future.

GOLDEN MORNING: Hampton National Historic Site ▲
Early morning light gilds the golden leaves of autumn providing contrast for the Parterre Gardens of Hampton National Historical Site. With varied coloration setting the many specimen trees apart, fall is a beautiful time to visit.

FUCHSIA!: Cylburn Arboretum ◄
In the All-American Display Garden in Cylburn Arboretum, these asters stand in glorious array. They are beautiful candidates for the gardens of visitors interested in flowers to brighten up the late summer garden.

HAYSTACK: Aᴍᴇʀɪᴄᴀɴ Iɴᴅɪᴀɴ Gᴀʀᴅᴇɴ ▲

Lying in the summer sun alongside an edge of the woods behind a "long-house", the Indian Garden speaks eloquently of the limitations of Indian agriculture. Corn in scraped-up mounds of shallow topsoil is subject to the vagaries of the weather, competition of other wild plants, and predation of wildlife.

CABBAGES AND MARIGOLDS: Gᴏᴅɪᴀʜ Sᴘʀᴀʏ Pʟᴀɴᴛᴀᴛɪᴏɴ Gᴀʀᴅᴇɴ ▶

Entry to the garden of the Godiah Spray Plantation is through the gateway of a primitive picket fence made of thin slabs of felled logs. Fences around early gardens guarded against spoilage from the owner's poultry and livestock as well as wildlife.

COMPANIONS: Margaret Brent Garden ▲
Young crepe myrtle and geraniums join with honored inhabitants of an 1850's formal garden. Boxwood, over 100 years old, stand companionably with their new neighbors.

PINK SNAPDRAGONS AND PICKET FENCE: Farthing's Ordinary Garden ▶
A picket fence made of thin slabs of wood surrounds Farthing's Ordinary Garden. It keeps the kitchen and dessert gardens safe from the intrusion of browsers as it would have in the time of the early colonists. Oyster shells, a common commodity for the residents of early St. Mary's City, provide dry footing in the garden.

YARROW AND FRIENDS: St. Mary's College Herb Garden ▶▶
Yellow yarrow stands above pink yarrow in companionship with blue hyssop and silvery lamb's ears. Tidily arrayed in beds set apart by sidewalks, this herb garden is at the St. Mary's College. Its beauty lies in the design of the garden and the luxurious growth of the plants.

that cares for it. If the health of the support falls off, the health of the garden does also. Gardens after all are living entities.

The book is divided into seven chapters, grouping the gardens according to interest. **In the Shadow of the Capitol** covers three gardens in and around Annapolis, the elegant, the hidden and the beautiful. **Baltimore's Best–Four Gardens** moves from the center of town at the conservatory through a single-season garden, an arboretum, and finishes with an historic site outside of the Beltway. **Gardens of the Past and Present in St. Mary's City** involves eight gardens and an insight into the role of archaeology in garden restoration. **Town and Country Living** takes the visitor out of the metropolis to see a variety of gardens from Carroll County in the middle of the state to Talbot County on the eastern shore and as far south as St. Mary's County. **Specialties** is a group of gardens, each having a distinctive feature about it: a biblical garden, a garden for butterflies, two azalea gardens with such a contrast in planting philosophy that they are handsomely different, and a water lily garden that is known nationwide. Last, but far from least, is the internationally known topiary garden of Harvey Ladew. **Two for a Day** presents gardens in pairs that lend themselves to combined excursions. For the most part, they are far enough from the rest of the state that combining the garden visits provides for very satisfactory day trips. For information on the gardens according to county, access for the handicapped, acreage, and other facts, see Appendix A. Appendix B is a list of dedicated volunteers whose efforts are greatly appreciated by the gardens. Appendix C provides tips and a checklist for trips to assist the reader in preparing for a solo journey or a bus trip for a group of friends.

Finally, special notice should be given to one plant which is not in a garden. Neither did it have its growth at the hands of man. While historic trees at Hampton national historic site have particular significance, it is impossible to talk of significant Maryland trees without including the Wye Oak at Wye Mills in Talbot County. The ages of the yew trees at Mount Harmon in Cecil County and the Cedar of Lebanon at Hampton have been remarked upon, but they are only youngsters when compared to the Wye Oak. This is the best known tree within the state. Many citizen gardeners have a Wye seedling planted in their yards. One young Wye Oak sapling stands in the garden at the Carroll County Farm Museum. During the course of its long life, the Wye Oak has gained a crown of more than 160 feet supported by a massive trunk girded about with supporting knees. This white oak tree in Talbot County is a symbol of survival as it approaches its 450th birthday.

Agriculture provides food for the body, but gardening provides food for the spirit. Visit these gardens in good health and good spirit.

CHAPTER TWO

In the Shadow of the Capitol

Annapolis, capital of Maryland, home of the Naval Academy, and host to thousands every year, is graced with 350 years of history. The natural barriers of the Severn River, the Chesapeake Bay, and a busy dock restrict expansion along two sides of the city. When you add the inflow of traffic to the state office buildings, it is no wonder that parking is at a premium and that the streets are filled with hustle and bustle.

Its population as well as its houses are compressed. Its residents and their visitors escape to the bay for a bit of beauty and space. They also retreat close at hand for that same peace, space, and beauty.

Within a five-mile radius of the city of Annapolis are three of the state's public gardens with multiple attractions: the pleasure gardens of William Paca, the Helen A. Tawes memorial garden, and the arboretum of the London Town Publik House. Parterre gardens, shaded walks, quiet pools, gleaming footbridges, and a presence of history combine to make these gardens islands of beauty.

The Pleasure Gardens of William Paca

Combed and parted

Within the intersecting, angled streets of Annapolis is Paca House with all of its history and loveliness. Built originally by William Paca, third governor of Maryland, in the mid-1760s, this 37-room mansion is accompanied by a 2-acre, picturesque-styled garden. A small spring-fed, fish-shaped pond lies at the back of the garden and can be crossed by a dainty white bridge leading to a pavilion.

Both the Paca House and the garden exist today as restorations. The restorations at the hands of dedicated archaeologists and the Historic Annapolis, Inc. group have brought forth a garden such as William Paca might have trod. While strolling the paths, beholding the roses, and crossing the "Chippendale" bridge, it is easy to imagine the enjoyment William Paca and his family had with this garden.

This garden is the most formal of all the public gardens of Maryland and one of the

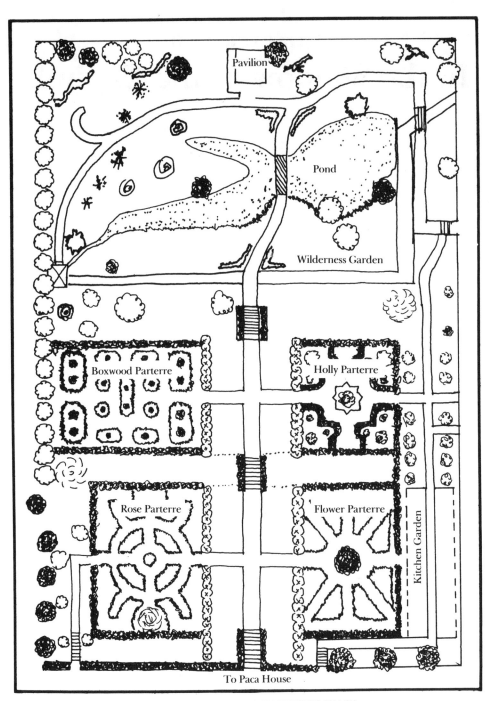

PLEASURE GARDENS OF WILLIAM PACA

most beautifully kept. Gravel walks raked to perfection, raised beds of kitchen garden, arbor-covered walks, and enclosed specialty gardens are at every turn. Parterres, in pairs, step stately down the slope. The four main parterres are the boxwood parterre, the holly parterre, the flower parterre, and the rose parterre. These four gardens lie along either side of the *Grand Allee,* two by two.

At the end of the *Grand Allee* is the pavilion, focal point of view. A small two-story house with a dome on top, it appears as a visual counterweight to the mass of the Paca House at the other end of the garden. It sits amid the wilderness garden in a light informal setting as contrasted to the heavier, precise formal gardens near the Paca House. The wilderness garden surrounds the fish-shaped pond that has waterside plants in residence. Lizard's-Tail's white blossoms grace a drooping spike, Cardinal Flower's scarlet blossoms provide a sharp contrast in color, Pickerelweed sends its blue flower stalk straight up, and the Fringed Loosestrife presents its sunny yellow. Button Bush, Flowering Raspberry, Beauty Berry, and Bottlebrush Buckeye join the Swamp Magnolia in filling out the color scheme of the wilderness garden.

The gardens can be viewed on a seasonal basis without tiring the visitor because of changes in bloom and coloration. All of the plants currently in the gardens are true to those that might have been found in William Paca's garden. All of the roses bloom in a single season in May. Their beauty is rivaled only by their fragrance. Standing over an inviting garden bench within the rose parterre is a Golden Rain tree that sports light green pods after the shower of yellow blossoms is gone. Truly, the visitor will feel a call to sit a spell and enjoy the morning.

Three-tiered topiaries of English variegated holly join American holly in the holly parterre for year-round beauty. In the flower parterre, eight smaller parterres enclose finely bladed grass surrounded by colorful leaves and blossoms from early spring until hard frost. Purple leaves of Prince's Plume, zinnias with their summer colors, and Globe Amaranth crisp in its magenta array intermingle with the airy lightness of white Baby's Breath within their bordered beds, while blue *Agapanthus africanus* stand tall in their large urns.

Forest green leaves with crisp smooth surfaces form a backdrop for the cream-white petals of the *Magnolia grandiflora*. This beautiful specimen magnolia tree on the Paca House terrace and a white crape myrtle tree stand guard over the large pots holding lantana spaced along the edge of the terrace.

Annapolis visitors will need the better part of the morning or afternoon to see the Paca Garden. The steps and gravel walks are the only drawback; they do not lend themselves to the handicapped visitor. To take in the garden and house on the same trip is possible. However, it would not do justice to either one. This garden is so filled with history, style, information, and beauty that it is highly recommended for repeat visits.

Helen Avalynne Tawes Garden

State sampler

What can be done with a flat, barren, cinder parking lot? More than you might think. After the erection of a box canyon formed by the Maryland State Office Buildings, the landscape architects were faced with a 6-acre rectangle enclosed with glass and marble multistoried office buildings on three sides (Rowe Boulevard comprised the fourth). The ugly remaining center had to be landscaped. The problem was not small. The solution became an award winner in the 1982

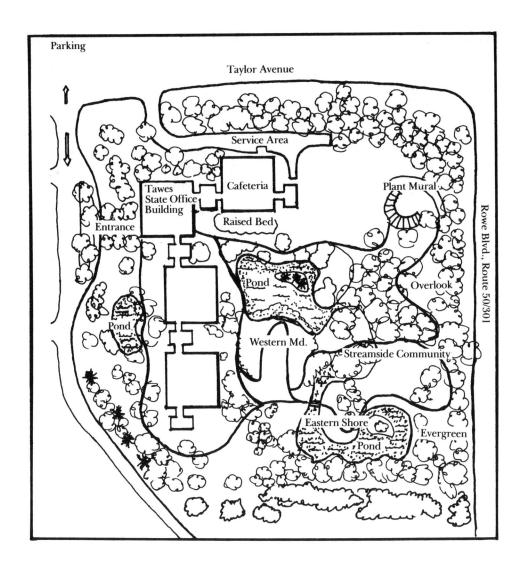

HELEN AVALYNNE TAWES GARDEN

American Landscape Architects' awards program, design division.

The Helen Avalynne Tawes Garden, named in honor of a former first lady of Maryland, is quite surprising when the surroundings are considered. The design is a patchwork sampler of habitats from Maryland; it is traversed by a serpentine walk that leads from one section to the next. Barrels of annuals sit along the walk. Each one is an overflowing arrangement of color chips in a bed of green. Centered by a series of mini-finger-lakes (ponds), the gardens range from a formal perennial garden to the natural setting of a brookside, and from the forest of the western mountains to the eastern shore.

While not a dedicated garden for the handicapped, the path's inclines are the most available to wheelchair visitors of any of the gardens visited. In fact, the first of the gardens, a "garden of the senses," was created in raised beds so that those in wheelchairs might be able to touch, taste, and smell the plants, many of which are herbs.

One small cul-de-sac lies in the open and allows a more formal arrangement of perennial flowers that need the longer periods of full sun. The early summer sun beams down on day-lilies of soft beauty as they open their short-lived blossoms. Like a patchwork quilt, the different flowers in this bed rise to bloom and then give way to another in a progression of color throughout the growing season.

A visitor pausing at a small bridge over a trickling stream will enjoy seeing the delicate spider-form pink of the *Rhododendron nudiflorum*, the wild azalea, during the early spring. Growing on the stream bank, it is an ideal woodland resident. The different levels of altitude of the ponds provide a slight current; the tiny falls and streams between the ponds trickle and splash in pleasant conversation.

Moving into the woodland area representative of the mountains of western Maryland, the visitor may spot wild flowers along the gravel walk during the early spring while the breeze rustles the needles of the evergreens overhead. Bloodroot, jack-in-the-pulpit, and hepatica raise their blossoms to the spring sun.

The peace and tranquility of the garden are reflected in the fact that a blue and a green heron routinely arrive to fish among the mallards who live in the ponds. Squirrels reside in the trees and more than 40 different birds have been spotted making a visit. For a city garden, its wildlife is thriving.

Many city office workers take their lunch to a park bench to eat, but how lucky are those who can stroll in this garden during their mid-day break. From the earliest bloodroot blossoms in the spring to chrysanthemums in the fall, color is everywhere. Shelter from the winds provided by the buildings makes this a garden that can be comfortably visited during its winter beauty. Stark outlines of the leafless trees are highlighted by fallen snow and softened by the grace of their needled evergreen neighbors.

Wide paths liberally dotted with benches invite the visitor to stay a while, listen to birdsong, visit with the squirrels, watch the mallards herd their convoys of young in and out of the banks of the ponds, and shed the stress of the day in doing so. This is not a garden to hurry through. It is a garden to sit in.

Within the garden it is hard to remember that beyond the fourth side of the garden traffic streams past.

Six acres is not much land, but the development has been excellent. The interlacing of paths, different levels of altitude, and different types of habitat allow the repeat visitor the luxury of being in a different garden from time to time. Growing and developing as the plants within it, the garden saw a groundbreaking for a new extension for the dunes of the eastern shore in 1986, to mark the tenth birthday of the garden.

Evolving for over 10 years, the garden is well worth a visit. Plan to take a lunch or snack and your camera, and plan to stay a while. This surely is a repeat garden.

The Arboretum of the London Town Publik House

Where the Past and Present Meet

South of Annapolis in Edgewater, Maryland, lie the remnants of London Town. It was once a thriving seaport town in the early 1700s and covered about a hundred acres. In 1863, it was designated as a port for the important shipping of tobacco. Located midway between Williamsburg and Philadelphia, London Town was also a good stopping point for north/south travelers. London Town Publik House served as an inn for such travelers — George Washington, Benjamin Franklin, and Thomas Jefferson — to name some of the more notable guests. As time went by, it became a meeting house for the public and later an almshouse for the poor.

Rescued from gradual decline, the Publik House was registered as a national historic landmark in 1970. The adjoining land, a veritable jungle, was painstakingly carved out to provide an arboretum dedicated to the display of native plants interspersed with immigrant plants. In our bicentennial year, the Garden Club of America gave national recognition to the arboretum at London Town.

If the Publik House had its illustrious guests, the garden has also had its share of distinguished visitors. J. D. Bond (Keeper of the Gardens, The Great Park — Windsor, England) visited in 1984. His impression was most favorable:

> I really was impressed with . . . the high standard that you are maintaining, coupled with a very good range of plants which were far better than most gardens that I visited in the U.S.

Beginning at the visitor's center, the early summer visitor is greeted by day-lilies swaying with the breeze and glowing with rich colors in the sun. This is a wonderful welcome to the garden. The path meanders past the day-lily beds, through spring walk, along winter walk, past the viburnum to Overlook Terrace. The layout of the garden is layered. Not only does the land undulate beneath the growth, but the landscape includes woods, lawn, and salt marsh. A boardwalk winds through the salt marsh along South River turning up along Almshouse Creek and returning to Overlook Terrace.

After leaving the terrace, the path passes wildflower walk and pauses at the meditation area. Descending stairs, the path proceeds through the azalea glade to the pond. In the pond, yellow and white water lilies nestle beside stately pink lotus blossoms. Among the flowers, damselflies follow a complex pattern back and forth. An earlier season finds Japanese iris, their feet happily situated in the damp pond side, raising their magnificent blossoms above slender stalks.

From below, near the pond, the view toward South River presents a vignette with slopes and trees framing the sight of the river beyond. Once again, ascending stairs beyond the pond, the path passes a new overlook. Looking down from the second overlook terrace, the visitor is captivated by the grass bowl containing the small stream-fed pond with its wooden bridge. This is the

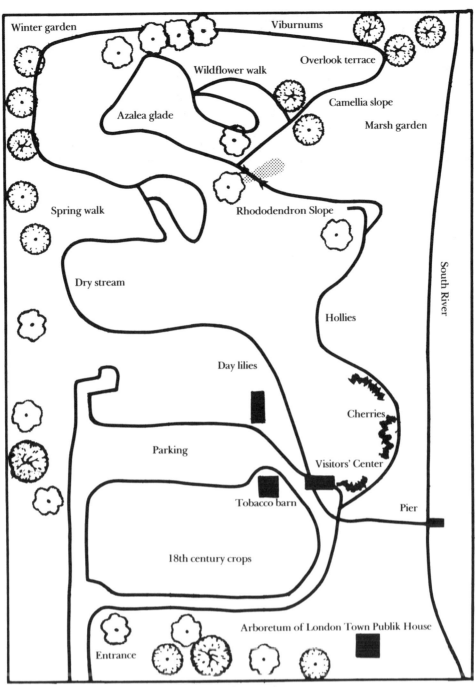

Winter garden

Viburnums

Wildflower walk

Overlook terrace

Azalea glade

Camellia slope

Marsh garden

Spring walk

Rhododendron Slope

South River

Dry stream

Hollies

Day lilies

Cherries

Parking

Visitors' Center

Tobacco barn

Pier

18th century crops

Arboretum of London Town Publik House

Entrance

LONDON TOWN

most beautiful scene in the garden. Continuing, the path threads through the rhododendrons, passing by the cherry trees, and returning to the visitor's center.

Rhododendrons and camellias grace the lower slopes nearest the river, while hybrid camellias are situated along the ridge above Almshouse Creek. Native trees, shrubs, wild flowers, and ferns have been given a special emphasis while cultivars and bulbs from other lands have been planted to complement the native species. There are also perennial shrubs, herbs, and 18th century crops. Between the herb garden and the 18th century crops stands a weathered log tobacco barn. Symbolic of tobacco as a cash crop in Maryland's history, it now serves as a tobacco exhibit center.

If masses of color are impressive, of equal if not greater delight in this garden are those extra-early or extra-late specimens, eye-catching because of their solo appearance. Long after most of the azaleas are gone, a Flame Azalea shouts for the attention of the visitor. Standing in an island of green, it benefits from less competition.

Magnolias with all of their variations shine in the warm spring light. During the early summer, the visitor is treated to the sight of *Hydrangea anomala* subsp. petiolaris, the Climbing Hydrangea. Two specimens climb trees at the southwest corner of the winter garden between the spring walk and winter garden. Nearly salad-plate-sized inflorescent blooms stud the air about the vine with floral snowflakes when in bloom. In and around all of these trees, shrubs, and flowers, tying the whole together, are plantings of ferns.

For the visitor who seeks the less favored, but still interesting, wild plants; a haze of orange color among the marsh plants whispers for attention. Examination reveals a growth of pale orange Dodder twining up the stalks, complete with minuscule white flowers.

It is fitting that a garden full of living, growing things is in itself growing. The gardens had already expanded from eight acres to nine, when clearing began in the winter of 1985-86 for the final fourteen acres. Plans are underway for new buildings. In the future there will be complete facilities for the handicapped.

Special exhibits are also presented in the visitor's center. The programs and exhibits are centered around colonial times and reflect the heritage of Anne Arundel County.

Small, a bit hard to find, and not widely known, the garden is well worth seeking out. Although finding the garden is not easy, abundant plant material, cool inviting walks, stairs, promontories, and the lovely little pond guarantee that the visitor will return.

NOTES AND DIRECTIONS

Pleasure Gardens of William Paca

Hours: M - Sat., 10 a.m.-4 p.m.; Sun., 12 noon-5 p.m.; May - October. 12 noon-4 p.m.; November - April

Season: May through November (open all year)

Services: Tours

Admission: Fee

Information: Gardens and house are closed on Thanksgiving and Christmas. The house is closed on Monday. This garden is marginally adequate for the handicapped. It is not a good garden for the wheelchair-bound visitor. The walks are gravel and there are steps. Call to arrange tours.

Phone: (301) 267-6656 or (301) 269-0601

Directions:

From Annapolis:

From Route 50 take Rowe Blvd. (Route 70). On Rowe Blvd., proceed inward to College Ave. Turn left on College Ave. Proceed to King George, turn right on King George, and continue to East Street. Just before East Street you will pass the back of Paca House. (You may enter the gardens through the house which faces Prince George's St.) At East Street, turn left for a block and then turn right on Martin Street. Enter through the Visitors' Center on Martin Street.

Parking Notes: Parking in Annapolis is at a premium. Be careful to note the parking restrictions on the street where you park. Ticketing is strictly maintained. Free parking is available at the Navy-Marine Stadium and shuttle buses run from the stadium to the historic district.

Helen Avalynne Tawes Memorial Garden

Hours: Daylight

Season: Spring to fall

Services: Guided tours

Admission: None

Information: There is easy access to most parts of the garden for wheelchair-bound visitors. Open year round even when the buildings are closed; however, *all rest rooms are within the buildings.*

A cafeteria adjacent to the patio is open to the public during the work week. Guided tours at no charge are available, reservations are required. A visitor's center is in the lobby of the Tawes State Office Building. It features an information center, displays, and a gift shop.

Although the garden is located in one of the most congested of areas, access to parking and this garden is very good. A good distance from the parking lot has to be covered. Parking is abundant. A shuttle bus runs from the parking lot to the building entrance. Drivers with handicapped may unload in the front drive and then go park.

Phone: (301) 974-3717

Directions:

From Annapolis:

From Route 50, exit on Rowe Boulevard toward Annapolis town center. At the intersection of Rowe and Taylor Ave. (Route 435), turn right. Turn right into the stadium parking lot.

If the vehicle carries handicapped visitors, turn left and having made a counterclockwise loop, discharge passengers in front of the Tawes State Office Building before parking.

London Town Publik House and Garden

Hours: T - Sat. 10 a.m. — 4 p.m.; Sun., Noon-4 p.m. Closed Monday and the months January and February.

Season: Spring through fall.

Services: Tours, weddings by prior arrangement

Admission: Fee

Information: School and tour groups should call for rates and information on special programs.

Phone: (301) 956-4900

Directions:

By car:

From Washington:

Take Route 50 toward Annapolis. Turn south on Route 424 (Davidsonville Rd.) to Route 214 east (Central Ave). Turn left on Stephney's Lane. Stephney's Lane becomes Londontown Rd. Drive to end of road.

From Baltimore:

Take Route 2 toward Annapolis. Continue to Edgewater and turn left on Mayo Rd. After 1 mile on Mayo Rd., turn hard left on Londontown Rd. (easy to miss). Drive to end of road.

By boat:

Take South River, opposite Buoy 15. Continue between Almshouse Creek and Glebe Creek 6 miles from the Chesapeake Bay. Dockage free for visitors to the Publik House and Garden; deep draft boats can also be accommodated.

CHAPTER THREE

Baltimore's Best–Four Gardens

Baltimore is blessed with four diverse, beautiful public gardens, most of which are accessible by public transportation, allowing visitors without automobiles to see them. These gardens range from several blocks to 176 acres and from the single season garden, such as Sherwood Garden's tulips, to the conservatory which is beautiful for the entire year. Working from the center of the city to the edges of the metropolitan area, the progression of gardens leads from the City of Baltimore Conservatory to Sherwood Gardens, on to the Cylburn Arboretum, to a finale at the Hampton National Historic Site just outside of the Beltway.

City of Baltimore Conservatory

Museum of life

Along the edge of Baltimore's Druid Hill Park stands an intriguing structure of glass reminiscent of a tintype of the 1900s. It appears anachronistic when viewed with 20th-century automobiles parked in front of it. Built in 1888, the Palm House of the Conservatory is an antique among the gardens of Maryland. It is accompanied by three greenhouses which contain orchids, desert plants, and display plants. It is ideal as a retreat from the grey and gloom of winter. The Conservatory of Baltimore gives winter-weary visitors the hope that spring cannot be far away. The beauty of the poinsettias, the heavy scent of a blooming gardenia, and the exotic look of the orchids are only the beginning of the offerings of the conservatory. of the conservatory.

Within the elegant structure of the Palm House of the conservatory, banana trees stand toe to toe with palms, both of which are graced about the base with ferns. All are interspersed with bulbous flowering plants. A statue of a girl and a water pool lend an air of tranquility to the greenery. Bougainvillaea ascend the glass wall to bloom on high, while nearby, the Fish Tail Palm is laden with the characteristic "fish tail" fruits. A beckoning scent leads around one corner and then another until the blooming gardenia is located; the plant is rather small but commanding in its fragrance.

All conservatories are plagued by the constraints of space. Plants do grow up and out, divide, and multiply. Space that once was adequate is no longer plentiful. It is so in the

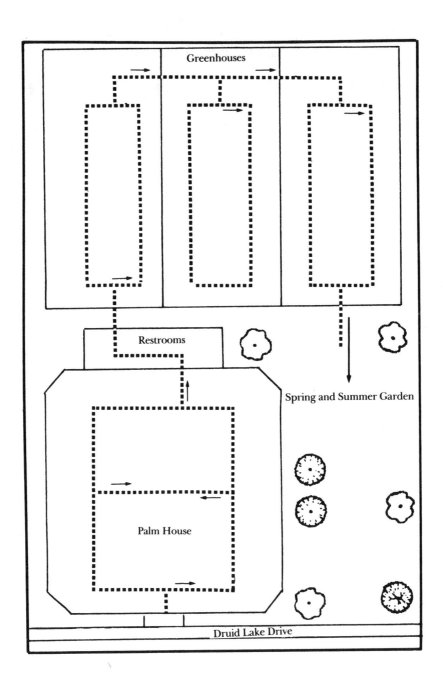

CITY OF BALTIMORE CONSERVATORY

Palm House, the largest structure of the conservatory. Like the bougainvillaea that climbs the glass, the palms reach ever higher, dominating the room, promoting the feeling that here the visitor is indeed in a tropical setting. Most of the plants in the Palm House are from the tropic or semitropic regions. Norfolk Island Pines contribute to the green-wall effect.

The mostly green setting makes a delightful backdrop for the pots of holiday-specific display plants. At Christmas time poinsettias of red, white, and pink display their holiday finery. As the seasons rotate, poinsettias are followed by the spring array of daffodils, tulips, lilies, hyacinths, primroses, and cineraria dazzling in their display.

For those who love plants, or for those who do not know them, this is an educational stop. Within the expected, the visitor finds the unexpected and return visits reveal new offerings. Education that is delightful, however, is no pain at all.

Summer visitors may walk among the outdoor beds as well as under the glass. Fall is dominated by chrysanthemums, but winter has to be the finest season in the conservatory. The contrast of the weather outside and the pleasant warmth inside combined with the odor of damp earth, growing plants, and blooming flowers lingers in the visitor's memory to be recalled again and again.

Sherwood Gardens

Seeing your tulips and planting them too

The hobby of John W. Sherwood was growing tulips. Few people have the funds to indulge their hobby so well. A petroleum pioneer and conservationist, John Sherwood may well be remembered best for his bequest of the Sherwood Gardens when he died in 1965. Because Mr. Sherwood left only enough funds to care for the gardens for one year, other arrangements had to be made for the gardens to continue. In 1966 the Guilford Association and the City of Baltimore assumed joint responsibility for its upkeep.

The big advantage of a city garden is, of course, its accessibility. It is not necessary to have a car to enjoy the beauty of Sherwood Gardens. Looking at Sherwood Gardens at their peak, one could almost think he or she was in Holland. Eighty thousand tulips of almost every imaginable color bloom in beds dotting the six acres. No paths cross this garden, just a broad expanse of lawn. Along the edge of the garden at different intervals are large stately private homes, their lawns flowing down to meet and blend into the beauty of Sherwood.

In addition to the beauty of the spring bloom time, the garden has a secondary benefit. Each year after the tulips have died back and are ready to be dug, a day is set aside when anyone who wishes to have some of these beautiful tulips may go "dig" at a very minimal charge per bulb. Diggers may have as many as they are willing to dig, pay for, and carry away.

Remember, there are sidewalks around the perimeter but none crossing through the gardens, so access is limited. No facilities exist. A beautiful park for ten months of the year, Sherwood Gardens shines in the sun for a month in the spring.

Cylburn Arboretum

. . . environmental education and horticulture

"Springtime is the time to see Cylburn," is repeated often by those who have seen it. Located off Northern Parkway West and Cylburn Avenue, this quiet arboretum could escape notice behind its fence. Set well back in the grounds of the 176-acre site, it cannot be seen from the street.

Intended to be the home of wealthy businessman/importer Jesse Tyson and his mother, the building of Cylburn was interrupted by the Civil War. The mansion, however, was finished in time for the arrival of his bride, Edyth, and it remained private property until their deaths. Upon Edyth's death in 1942, the city bought the property for a city park. Today, the city's horticultural headquarters are now housed within the mansion.

While it might be possible to reach the arboretum by public transportation, the visitor should know that this is an area of large dimensions. If they arrive without a car, there is a lot of walking to do. However, the park-like atmosphere free from traffic invites the visitor to walk, jog, or ride a bike.

Cylburn is a mid-city arboretum with a lot of the countryside retained. City dwellers can have a taste of the out-of-doors and feel a bit of freedom of space. There is room to move about without rubbing elbows with others. Close at hand, it allows repeat visits. If visitors return often enough they may find themselves in the volunteer line, digging in the dirt, planting, and giving the gift of beauty to others.

Inside the gate, the drive passes through a tree-studded lawn on its way back to a small parking lot just before arriving in front of the mansion. Volunteer groups have taken on the responsibility for care of the different gardens lying behind the mansion, the most significant of which are The All-American Selections Display Garden, the Shade Garden, and the Perennial Garden.

In front of the mansion within the circular drive stands an enormous footed urn of cast iron filled with bedding plants. Lawn encircles the urn which in turn has a perimeter of

bedding plants creating a striking beginning for the garden.

When wild flowers grace the Wildflower Walk, it will not be long before tulips, daffodils, and other spring bulbs dance across the lawns in the springtime creating a wonderland of color. The abundance of trees within its arboretum makes Cylburn an autumn collage, but the stark beauty of the leafless trees during winter can only be appreciated by a true outdoorsman.

Cylburn in the summer is different from all of the rest of the year. In summertime, Cylburn gardens provide a place of retreat and peace within the busy clamor of the city. Once inside the gates, the traffic disappears, the sun shines warmly, and the shade invites the visitor to stop awhile, park the car, and go afoot.

The small Shade Garden, a memorial to Paulene E. Waters, is directly behind the mansion and between the mansion and the All-American Selections Display Garden. It lies, tree-shaded, within a picket fence. The garden holds hosta lilies, calla lilies, and violets amid boxwood beneath shade trees. Cool stone benches await the weary or meditative. A broad brick path curves from one gate to the other leading the visitor through the small garden and on to the display garden.

The All-American Selections Display Garden contains the best of the old along with new varieties. Here the visitor may see the newest members of the annuals: snapdragons, marigolds, petunias, asters, and zinnias; these are only a few of the varieties grown in 200 display gardens throughout the country.

Display gardens are used to test the viability and reproduction of new varieties of plants before they are put on the market. Prior to their being sent to display gardens, they are tested in university test plots across the nation. At the end of their year stay in the test plots, they are judged and, in worthy cases, awards are made by the All-American Selections organization. The organization was begun in 1932 by W. Ray Hastings for the purpose of testing and evaluating new seeds. The All-American Selections have been joined by the All-American Rose Selections and the All-American Gladiolus Selections. Upon receipt of their status as an All-American Selection, seeds are sent by the seed company to the display gardens for the new year.

In beds of 2-1/2 by 4-feet long in a garden about a quarter of an acre, these new plants and some of the old favorites grow on display, presenting a checkerboard riot of color in the middle of the summer. For specimens being tested, seed is counted and compared with the rate of germination; the growth of the plants is documented; and the amount of bloom or size of the vegetation or fruit or other edible portion is recorded. The plant's ability to cope with different weather and soil conditions in different areas in the country is documented. This information is collated prior to bringing the new variety out on the market. During June, July, and August, three reports are sent from the display garden to the company having supplied the seed under scrutiny. A variety that is sensitive to conditions in too many parts of the country might not be marketable. From that information will come decisions as to which varieties will be best to put on the market in the near future.

Active gardeners are always looking for new plants to put into their own garden. In the wintertime they peruse the catalogs as fast as the postman brings them to the door. A visit to a display garden such as Cylburn, in full riot of bloom in the summer, is ever so much better. It is a living wishbook for the gardener who likes to wander through the pages of garden catalogs.

Alongside of the display garden is the perennial garden with a collection of tree peonies. An isle between boxwood hedges is bordered by beds filled with a host of different perennials. Summer bloom provides splashes of color against the green backdrop. A garden of the senses is being restored; it is hoped that it will be ready for the sight-impaired as well as the wheelchair-bound visitors in the spring of 1988. Add to these special gardens, wild flower walks and acres of peaceful tree-sprinkled grounds and you have a living treasure within reach of the city's inhabitants as well as a magnetic attraction for visitors from out of town.

Hampton National Historic Site

Choice proven by the test of time

North of Towson and just outside the Baltimore Beltway is the Hampton National Historic Site. At the time the mansion was built (1783-1790), it was far from the acceptable sites for wealthy homes and not as safe as it could be. Rather isolated, it was therefore known by some as "Ridgely's Folly." The presence of wolves and the absence of gentry, however, did not deter Captain Charles Ridgely. He lavishly spent his money from iron ore to build and maintain this massive mansion in spite of the opinions of his peers.

Captain Charles Ridgely, the builder, was one of several generations of enterprising Ridgelys. He gained his wealth through the capitalization of large deposits of iron ore in Baltimore County. Wealth from the iron ore continued in the family for 100 years after his death. With his wealth he accumulated property in Baltimore County and Harford County. At one time he could ride across 27 miles of his own land. The size of the house is in keeping with the land he owned. Georgian

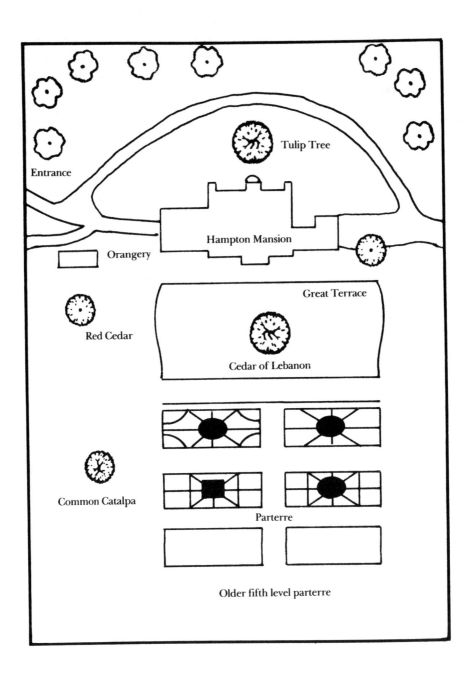

HAMPTON NATIONAL HISTORIC SITE

in style, the house's architecture has been criticized as being that of an amateur; the wings are diminutive in relationship to the general mass and the porticos too bulky. The whole was capped with a majestic cupola once thought to be inspired by the octagonal dome on Castle Howard in England.

The mansion and garden were built with plans so carefully made that the finished four-level gardens appear as though the on-looker was seeing a living tapestry from the cupola. The mansion remained in the family until 1948 when the estate was purchased by the Avalon Foundation for presentation to the United States Government as a national park.

The gardens of Hampton National Historic Site cannot be absorbed in the space of one morning or afternoon. The placement of the parterre gardens, south, and directly behind the mansion, would allow a clear view of them from the mansion except for the presence of a Cedar of Lebanon. In front of the mansion, a tree-lined drive arrives from Hampton Lane and circles around in front of the portico inscribing a heart design. East of the mansion is currently an herb garden, while to the west is the orangery. The parterre gardens, orangery, and an informal adaptation of English Landscape Park are worthy of several hours of contemplation.

While the construction of the parterres were by Captain Charles Ridgely, the development and construction of the gardens were under the hand of Charles Carnan Ridgely, Governor of Maryland, 1815-1818, and nephew of Captain Ridgely. Originally Charles Carnan, he made haste to have his name changed legally in accordance with the edict from his uncle's will in order to inherit the bulk of his uncle's estate. Hampton Mansion was inherited by Rebecca Ridgley, the captain's wife. She had life tenancy, but ex-

changed this right with Charles Carnan for other property in the area.

A filmstrip shown in the Information Center is a good beginning prior to viewing the gardens. The history of the house and gardens is laid out in detail and provides visual reference to the gardens during all seasons.

The orangery, a restoration, will be open in 1988 and serve as the Visitors' Center. The orangery housed one of America's best collections of citrus and provided grapes from vines espaliered along the walls. Originally, 40 orange trees, *Citrus chinensis*, lived within the orangery in the winter and lined the terrace during the summer. Commonly called the "sweet orange," *Citrus chinensis* would not appeal to modern taste since it would be considered entirely too sour. The reconstructed orangery still houses orange trees in wooden boxes in the winter.

The project of planting specimen trees was begun by Charles Carnan Ridgely. Among the list of notable trees in Maryland are several from Hampton National Historic Site. The most famous is the Cedar of Lebanon which has the honor of being the state champion. Several catalpas trees are nearly 200 years old.

Other trees of interest include the Saucer Magnolia, pecan, tulip, Purple European Beech, and Red Cedar. Younger trees of interest include the ginkgo with its fan-shaped leaves. In the fall, yellow runs in ribbon strips along the edges of the ginkgo leaves, ever widening until the entire leaf is emblazoned with gold.

The parterre gardens lie along levels of the earthen falls. They begin with the Great Terrace and descend to the second terrace by way of a grassed slope, then to the third terrace and finally on to the fourth level. Descending by way of grass slopes was a departure from the formal descent by steps or stairs. It was considered a most remarkable accomplishment of earth-work engineering in its time. Another engineering feat that is special at Hampton was the creation of a wooden pipe irrigation system (10,590 feet) to insure that all of the work put into the gardens would not fail in case of drought. The wooden pipe was later replaced with lead pipe.

The three lower levels make up the parterre gardens with formal plantings of intricate design. The first is a formal geometric design, the second a garden of heritage roses, and the third a garden of peonies. Each set of gardens is true to the planting arrangement of its origins. The Heritage Rose Garden joins in spirit with other gardens in saving for the future those plants of the past that retain strengths gradually eroding away from the plant gene-pool.

A panoramic display of the gardens can be viewed from the south side of the circular walkway of the Great Terrace. For those who are unable to see the parterre gardens up close, it should be a comfort to know that the gardens are most spectacularly enjoyed from a distance. This is a garden of grand design rather than micro-perfection.

Not all of the grounds are suitable for an enjoyable visit for the wheelchair-bound visitor. There is much to see, however, in the many acres of the gardens. Everyone should be able to have an enjoyable time. In addition to strolling and viewing the several parts of the gardens, the visitor may have luncheon in the tea room and buy gifts in the gift shop.

This is a very good garden for return visits. Every season will show a different garden. These gardens were built in the fashion of the 18th century for the contemplation of nature, and they succeed immeasurably. Spring and fall with their riot of color in many ways do more justice to the grounds than either summer or winter.

NOTES AND DIRECTIONS

City of Baltimore Conservatory

Hours: Daily, 10 a.m. - 4 p.m.

Season: Open year round

Services: Classes

Admission: None

Information: Space is at a premium within the conservatory. It is traversed by narrow paths, not the best for the wheelchair-bound visitor.

Phone: (301) 396-0180

Directions:

Baltimore:

Note: Major road construction was ongoing on the Jones Falls Expressway at the time of publication, 1987. A call would insure whether alternate routes should be selected.

From the Baltimore Beltway, take the Jones Falls Expressway toward town. The Druid Hill Park is alongside the Jones Falls Expressway between Gwynns Falls Parkway and McCulloh Street. The conservatory is on Druid Lake Drive.

Baltimore by public transportation:

Because public transportation changes so frequently in routes, times, and connections, contact the MTA office for pertinent information: (301) 539-5000

Sherwood Gardens

Hours: Daylight

Season: The garden is usually best at the end of April.

Admission: None

Information: Telephone ahead to ask about bloom and/or dig dates. Facilities are non-existent. The grounds would not be easy to traverse in a wheelchair. Since parking is not permitted along the street, it is very easy to have a lovely view driving around the garden.

Phone: (301) 366-2572

Directions:

From Baltimore:

From either the Baltimore Beltway or the center of town, Sherwood Gardens are about halfway between these two points on the northern extension of Charles Street. Stratford Road joins the west side of Charles Street about three streets north of 39th Avenue.

If the driver is facing north (out of town) at this point, Charles Street becomes one way going north and one way coming to this point from the north (at the left). Stratford is easy to miss if the driver is traveling from north to south.

Traveling from the center of town, bear right on Stratford Road. Cross St. Paul and approach Greenway. The lower west corner of the garden will be in front and to the right of the intersection.

Baltimore by bus:

Because public transportation changes so frequently in routes, times, and connections, contact the MTA office for pertinent information: (301) 539-5000

Cylburn Arboretum

Hours: Daily, 8 a.m.-4 p.m. Building open T - T, 10 a.m.-3 p.m.

Season: Grounds open 365 days of the year

Services: Group tours

Admission: None

Information: Facilities open from outside the building. Note: Not all areas of the grounds are readily accessible to the handicapped, but much of it is very approachable even via a wheelchair. Call for group tours.

Phone: (301)396-0180

Directions:

From Baltimore:

Note: Major road construction was ongoing on the Jones Falls Expressway at the time of publication, 1987. A call would insure whether alternate routes should be selected.

From the Baltimore Beltway (I-695), take Jones Falls Expressway (Route 83) south into Baltimore to Northern Parkway West. Turn left on Cylburn Avenue, left on Greenspring, and immediately left into the grounds.

Because public transportation changes so frequently in routes, times, and connections, contact the MTA office for pertinent information: (301) 539-5000

Hampton National Historic Site

Hours: Daily 9 a.m. - 5 p.m. Closed January 1, Thanksgiving, and December 25

Season: Spring through fall

Services: Tours available as are tearoom, gift shop, educational programs.

Admission: None (possible change, fall 1987)

Information: Arrange for group tours and tearoom in advance.

Phone: (301) 823 - 7054 or Tearoom (301) 583-7401

Directions:

From Baltimore:

From the Baltimore Beltway (I-695), take exit 27 (Dulaney Valley Road) or Exit 28 (Providence Road) north to Hampton Lane. From Dulaney Valley Road, turn right on Hampton Lane. This turn is easily confused with the ramp onto the Beltway. It is the first street *after* the ramp for the Beltway.

From Providence Road, turn left. Hampton Lane runs in front of Hampton National Historic Site.

CHAPTER FOUR

Gardens of the Past and Present in St. Mary's City First Capital of Maryland

Gardens, like the people who grow them, are individual in purpose and composition. Each one sports a different identity even when they are dedicated to the same plant groups. True in the past, true now, and true in the foreseeable future, this fact is observable in the gardens of St. Mary's City. Eight gardens lie in an interwoven tapestry and are nearly inseparable.

The gardens to be seen here represent the plain, the instructive, and the pretty. Beginning at Chancellor's Point and proceeding in a counterclockwise direction, a walking tour of the gardens of approximately two miles would progress from the American Indian Garden to the Freedom of Conscience Memorial Garden. The eight gardens are as follows:

- American Indian Garden
- Godiah Spray Plantation Garden
- Margaret Brent Memorial Garden
- Farthing's Ordinary Gardens
- St. Mary's College Herb Garden
- Mulberry Shoppe Herb Garden
- Garden of Remembrance
- Freedom of Conscience Memorial Garden

While spring is a lovely time to visit St. Mary's City, early to midsummer is the best time to see the entire array. Although the theme for each garden is different, plant types do overlap. Each garden has a link with history. Three are reconstructions based upon archaeological evidence. Three are dedicated to people and ideals of the past. Two are herb gardens and reflect the major roles that those plants have filled in the life of man.

While trails are available for those who like to hike, walking is not required as good roads join parking lots located at three central points from which the gardens at hand may be visited. The three main parking lots are at Chancellor's Point, Godiah Spray Plantation, and in front of Farthing's Ordinary. A fourth parking lot is located at the Visitors' Center. A system of trails to be completed by 1988 will join the outlying gardens.

The Role of the Archaeologists

Reconstructions are based upon what can be surmised from the physical evidence of the archaeologist's work and from reading the writings of the past. The American Indian Garden, the kitchen gardens of the Godiah Spray plantation, and of Farthing's Ordinary—an inn—are all reconstructions upon sites outside the St. Mary's excavation area. The reconstructions were developed by the St. Mary's City Commission.

Work of archaeologists reveals more than structures of houses, barns, or garbage pits. It entails digging into records, letters, diaries, and works of art to get a glimpse of the past. It also involves digging painstakingly into the soil to see what physical evidence it can reveal.

The court record of a claim for damages may show more about what an owner had planted in his garden than did his diary. An early artist's work speaks of what the archaeologist cannot physically find.

No evidence remains of the "long-houses" of the Piscataway Indians, one group of which lived in the St. Mary's City area. Even so, it is possible to reconstruct a "long-house" and plant a garden as it might have been in the 17th century.

Just as we send photographers today to a site of interest to obtain photographs, so in the 15th century were artists sent on voyages to sketch, paint, and thus record the evidence of what was found to be produced upon return to educate and delight those who did not go. John White was just such an artist. Thomas Harriot's *A Briefe and True Report of the New Found Land of Virginia* was published in 1588 and republished with the drawings of John White engraved by deBry in 1590. It was from examination of John White's drawings that the archaeologists were able to piece in much information on the Indians lost in time through physical decay.

Physical evidence of buildings and fences left behind by the earliest colonists of St. Mary's City is often easier to find and to draw conclusions from than plant material. After establishing the evidence of foundations of buildings and the distribution of artifacts revealing the use of those buildings, it then remains to speculation as to the use of the land portions nearby. Fence-prints at St. Mary's City, like footprints, tell the size and weight of the structure as well as the size of the enclosure. Three main types appear there: heavy fortification, medium defence such as picket fences, and less secure closely placed structures such as woven sapling fences. Pollen, the best evidence of plant types, unfortunately has not been found. It is fragile and requires optimum conditions to be preserved.

Once the archaeological evidence has been gathered, a theory is postulated. The theory would attempt to answer a two-part question to support a thesis. What physical evidence might the archaeologist be able to find? Where might it be found? The physical remnants unearthed, combined with the historical records, form an outline of what buildings and plantings probably existed at the site. From this data, plans may be made for the construction of a model of the site as it was in the past. The same kind of timbers and tools are used as would have been used in the past. In the case of gardens, only those seeds or plants which would have been used in the gardens in the past are planted in the reconstruction gardens.

Gardens have been the one place where written records to support the hypothesis of the contents of a garden are as absent as the physical evidence of the plants themselves. The only historical account occurred when Robert Cole documented his estate prior to his return to England and his subsequent death. The trustees of the estate kept the documentation up for an exceptional ten years, 1662 - 1672. It is upon such documentation that the Godiah Spray Plantation was

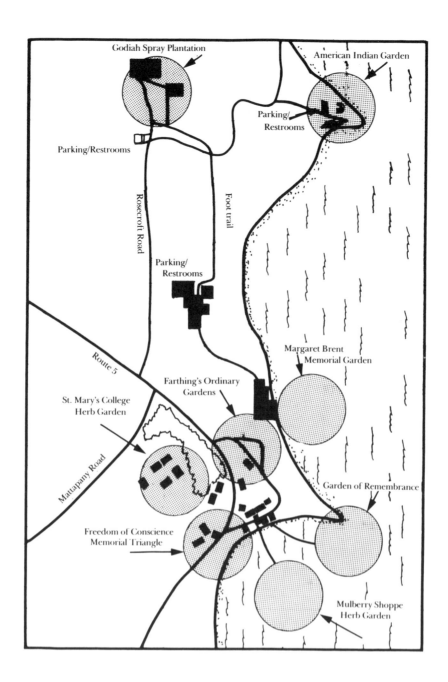

ST. MARY'S CITY

reconstructed. By examining the drawings of John White and other artists of the time and by drawing up a list of buildings and other garden uses of Robert Cole's estate, it was possible to set up an outline plan for the to-be reconstructed plantation. It was to be named Godiah Spray, a fanciful name reconstructed out of the common names of the period. This reconstruction involved names as common at the time as John Doe is today. *Farthing's Ordinary* was also a play on the word farthing (a piece of coinage) combined with ordinary, which was the word used for an inn.

The stark reconstruction of the Indian Garden is a subject for contrast of life style and philosophy between the colonists and the natives. The Indian Garden displays evidence of minimal attention, as the Indians did not own land. If drought came where they were, they simply went away leaving the garden to dry in the sun with little loss. The colonist owned his parcel of land and it in turn owned him. In bad times, both he and it suffered.

Reconstructed Gardens

The reconstructed gardens are products of the efforts by the St. Mary's City Commission to produce evidence of the City of St. Mary and to provide educational reconstructions for the benefit of the citizens of the present and the future. This is a growing heritage of an outdoor history museum that has been developing since 1974.

Today's visitors to St. Mary's City get a feeling of stepping into the past when they visit these reconstructed gardens. They are greeted by attendants, often theatrical students, dressed in colonial attire and speaking in accents of the past as they go about their work.

Memorial gardens and herb gardens

While the reconstruction gardens are dedicated to the gardens of the past, memorial gardens are dedicated to the memory of people of the past. In St. Mary's City there are three memorial gardens. In the first case, the Margaret Brent Garden is dedicated to a resident of colonial times, Margaret Brent, who was the first suffragette in the new world. In the second case, the Garden of Remembrance at St. Mary's College is dedicated to those of the more recent past who were connected with the college. Finally, one garden is dedicated to the concept of the Freedom of Conscience, an abstract concept memorialized in flowers and stone.

Two remaining gardens display the plants most prized to man. Visitors to St. Mary's City will enjoy viewing two distinct types of herb gardens. The College Herb Garden is a formal garden with a planned design for beauty and function, while the garden at the Mulberry Shoppe is closer to the kind of garden planted near a colonial wife's kitchen.

American Indian Garden

Lying in the summer sun behind a longhouse, the Indian Garden, an irregular plot of unplowed ground, approximately a third of an acre, speaks eloquently to the limitations of Indian agriculture. Corn, Jerusalem artichokes, and gourds planted in scraped-up mounds of shallow topsoil are subject to the vagaries of the weather, competition from other wild plants, and pillage by wildlife.

Maize (corn) was the most important of the crops. Typically, corn was eaten steamed in the husks or converted into hominy. Hominy was made by cooking the kernels of the corn in lye water for several hours to remove the coat of the kernel. When dried, the hominy could be ground and cooked with water to produce pone. Corn and beans cooked together made succotash. Gourds were another crop of use to the Indians. The fruit of the gourd had a number of applications. The hard thin shell of the gourd fruit formed a bowl with a ready supplied handle. A hole cut in one side of the fruit and with the seeds scraped out resulted in a ladle or bowl. Gourds of all sizes were used to spoon, dish, and hold water, ground meal, and hominy.

To walk among the mounds and consider that fresh vegetables for the summer, new utensils, bowls, and the vegetable needs of a coming winter depended upon the chance arrival of rain is a sobering thought. There are no fences here and no weeding. The garden path is a simple trail beaten down among the wild plants and grasses by the traffic of garden tenders. The Indians did have an advantage over the new settlers. They were not bound in place by ownership of land. When a season was not conducive to agriculture, they simply moved on.

Godiah Spray Plantation

The Godiah Spray Plantation garden is an interpretive garden representative of the 17th century. As in many vegetable gardens, the garden plot varies from year to year. Plants situated here this year will be moved to another site next year to help control diseases. Regardless of location, the garden contains greens (endive and spinach), peas, beans, cabbage, kohlrabi, onions, and garlic. Cucumbers for pickles and melons wind their way along edges of the beds. Sweet potatoes are given a good share of space for winter vegetables. Jerusalem artichokes, once implanted, were probably never eliminated as in gardens of today. Herbs were installed in their beds on a more permanent

basis and were the perennial residents of the garden.

The plants in the garden have their origins in the country of the owner or were borrowed from the Indians living nearby. The herb garden was mostly a transplant from home with additions from the Indians.

Entry to the garden of the Godiah Spray Plantation is through the gateway of a primitive picket fence made of thin slabs of felled logs. This entry seems appropriate after wending your way through rough-cleared fields. Corn and tobacco with their tree stump companions tell a clear story of the hard work it took to remove the forest from the ground to be planted.

Early gardens were guarded from the ravage of the owner's poultry and livestock as well as wildlife by a picket fence. The garden was fenced in, the animals kept out. The garden fed not only the immediate family, but also servants and slaves living on the plantation. However utilitarian it may have needed to be, it had its own beauty. In beds bordered by felled saplings, vegetables, herbs, flowers, and potherbs live in comfortable harmony with the same minimum of care that they would have had in the 17th century.

Farthing's Ordinary

Within the rough-fenced enclosure, seated beneath the arbor of the Ordinary, the visitor can easily imagine being a traveler from long ago seeking the whereabouts of the site granted to him to build upon. On one hand is the kitchen garden no more than a quarter of an acre. Dividing it from the dessert garden is an arbor with young grape vines. Tables and benches sit beneath the arbor. The dessert garden, nearly three times as large as the kitchen garden, is planted with young fruit trees and elderberry bushes, all of which supply food for the inn. A light lun-

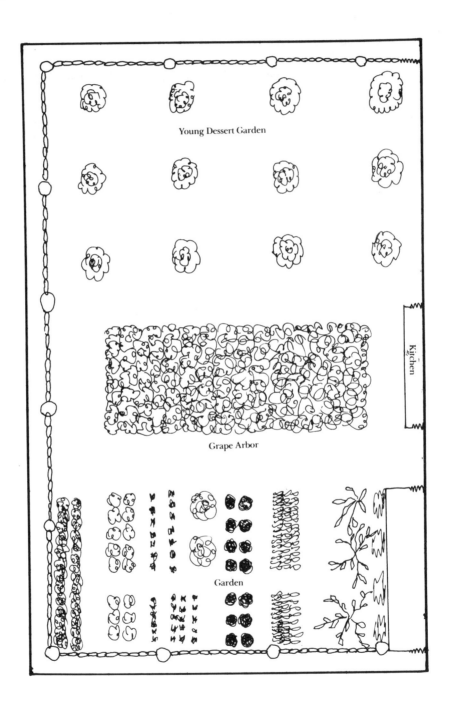

Young Dessert Garden

Grape Arbor

Kitchen

Garden

FARTHING'S ORDINARY

cheon featuring items flavored with the herbs at hand may be purchased as in days past. The dessert garden is young, but the presence of a few green, growing fruit trees promise that in the future peach or apple pies may well come from this source. The eager vines growing upward to the top of the arbor promise grapes glistening with morning dew.

The plants in the colonists' gardens had as many uses as possible. Vegetables, herbs, and flowers all found their places in the stew pot, apothecary, dye pot, or potpourri. The amount of energy required to carve out space for a garden demanded that it pay its way.

In lieu of seed catalogs, plants were permitted to go to seed and so it is today. We see onion heads with beautiful white balls of flowers, small delicate-pink balls sit atop chives. Because modern gardens are mostly harvested prior to seeding time, the beauty of common vegetable-flowers may be a surprise to visitors.

Herb Gardens

Two herb gardens grace this collection. Herbs for teas, medicinal purposes, dyes, or sachets often provide color to the garden as well as a delightful fragrance to the air. St. Mary's College and the Mulberry Shoppe both have herb gardens. The presence of an herb bed in each of the colonists' gardens, when there was not a garden devoted to herbs alone, attests to the importance of herbs in the lives of the people.

Some of the plant families give more generously to man than others. In the whole plant world, the *Gramineae* or grass family sustains humankind, but without herbs, it would be pretty dull eating. An herb is loosely defined as a plant that is useful to man, but this definition covers a lot of territory that is

not usually included in the word. Generally, herb is a designation of a group of plants which are small in character, without woody stems, fragrant in odor, and replete with oils of many uses. Many herbs have colorful flowers, and all have been used for centuries to flavor foods, help cure the hides of animals, sweeten houses prior to plumbing, dye cloth, poison the enemy, strengthen the sick, provide antibiotic to the injured, and insure happiness.

The St. Mary's College Herb Garden is petite, compact, and centered with a sundial. It was the recipient of the Governor's Cup for civic beautification in 1983. It is a fragrant spot in a hidden niche. Growing in a space no larger than a quarter of an acre with additional plantings of salmon-colored roses, this has to be one of the best demonstrations of concentrated herb gardening in the state. Walks work their way through the beds turning first one way and then doubling back, allowing the visitor close proximity to the specimens that are to be seen, smelled, and enjoyed. Bees and butterflies join in the parade visiting the flowers.

The Mulberry Shoppe Herb Garden is supported by the women of the Old Trinity Church and is a combination of bed and container plantings. Interspersed with rust-colored brick walks and contained by a rail fence, the garden is an invitation to enter and bide a bit. The Mulberry Shoppe herb garden fills all the space between the sidewalk and the street, little more than an overlarge parking strip. Concentrated though they are, the plantings make an attractive garden in miniature.

Margaret Brent Memorial Garden

In the winter of 1638, Margaret Brent, a member of the upper class in England, able to trace her lineage back to King Edward III, set foot on the dock of St. Mary's along with her sister and two brothers. Her sister was destined to fulfill the colonial woman's proper role. She married and raised a house full of children. Margaret would later have to take care of her sister and her sister's children when her brother-in-law had financial problems. Later, when he returned to England for a time, she again had to assume his responsibility for the family.

Margaret Brent denied the need to marry and proclaimed the right to keep the land she and her sister had been granted prior to their departure from England. This attitude certainly was in opposition to the colonial rule that demanded she marry and turn over the property to her husband. Although she was not a lawyer, she understood the law well enough to handle her estate's affairs as many of the landholders did. In time, not only would her brother-in-law use her legal abilities, but Margaret's brothers and many of the others in the community would also seek her assistance.

The proprietor of Lord Baltimore's landholding, upon his deathbed left the executorship of his estate in the capable hands of Margaret Brent with the unexplained statement "take all, pay all."[1] With this deathbed issuance of responsibility, Margaret Brent became a de facto Governor of Maryland for a short time. She quelled a riot caused by the army's not having been paid prior to the death of Lord Baltimore's proprietor. She gave financial assistance to individuals and representative assistance in court. The same Margaret Brent, however, was denied the right to a vote in the Maryland Assembly filled with many of the very men she had assisted more than once. These men cried shame that she should even think of such an idea.

Just as Margaret Brent was the first suf-

fragette of the new world and a most unusual woman for her time, the garden in her memory is also most unusual. As it covers archeological evidence of the past, many limitations were placed upon its creation. It is situated on the site of an original 1850's house garden and incorporates its existing boxwood. Permission to plant was required, digging was limited to six inches, and plants were restricted to an approved list. The result is one of openness and freedom which is significant in light of the freedom which Margaret Brent sought. This peaceful garden with broad lawn and restful benches includes a gazebo perched along the riverside allowing a view of the St. Mary's River, altogether a beautiful tribute to a most unusual lady.

Garden of Remembrance

Another garden overlooking the river, the Garden of Remembrance, is approximately a half-acre in an elongated rectangle. It is a formal garden of azaleas, dogwood, boxwood, crepe myrtle, and bedding plants.

Colleges are made up of people engaged in the serious pursuit of knowledge, from the greenest freshman to the most honored dean. All of those people have a need to get out-of-doors, let the breeze blow through their hair, and smell the flowers. The Garden of Remembrance provides just such a retreat from the pressures of the day.

In this small garden a grove of dogwood trees provides a lower layer of trees to their taller companions. The dogwood supply their beautiful white blossoms in the spring to celebrate the passing of winter, the examinations of the year, and the attainments of the graduates. Later in the fall, its bright red

---

[1]Susan E. Clagett, "Margaret Brent and the Town of Old St. Mary's," *The Baltimore Sun*, 18 October 1908.

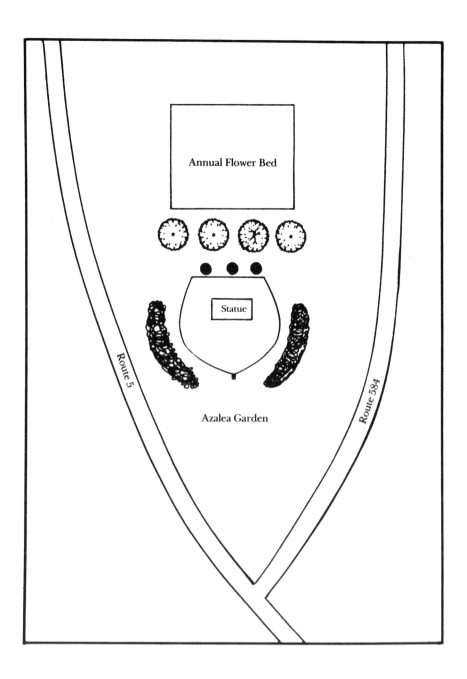

FREEDOM OF CONSCIENCE MEMORIAL TRIANGLE

berries and dusky red leaves accompanied with the tiny white minaret buds welcome the returning students and the time of harvest.

Summertime is a quiet time in the garden. The restful green of the boxwood is accented with tints and shades of pink supplied by the fluffy crepe myrtle. Birds talk among the trees and visit the small pool with its raised fountain. A leaf, fallen from a tree overhead, floats like a tiny craft on the water. At the outer edge of the garden, a walk underneath an arbor passes by benches. There the visitor may sit and watch water enthusiasts glory in the freedom of the wind and waves. The breeze is warm but welcome after the summer sun.

Beautiful during the spring, restful in summer, and brilliant during the fall, this garden provides walks, a fountain, and an arbor with benches to sit upon.

Freedom of Conscience Memorial Triangle

The Freedom of Conscience Memorial Triangle was established in St. Mary's City by all the counties of Maryland on the 300th anniversary of the founding of St. Mary's City.

The garden is centered by a statue with a walk and annual garden surrounding the base. The bright colors of the summer flowers glow as they bask in the sun. A relatively new azalea garden extends to the rear and is very attractive in the spring. Flags fly high above, to the rear of the statue.

The flowers are secondary in this garden for the statue dominates the scene. The more often it is contemplated the more admiration is given to the vision of the artist. As a representation of the freedom of conscience, it is significant that the figure cleaving its way up out of the stone is still held at the base by the stone from which it is emerging. Freedom is not easily won. The annuals and the statue are attractive during the summer season and the statue is impressive at all times.

This is a fitting close to the timeline the gardens are set upon. Each garden has marked the development of gardens and of the progress of man. Each has shown the steps taken to free his spirit of the encumbrances of toil, ignorance, and intolerance. In addition to the historic space they share, all of these gardens have another point in common. They are lovingly cared for by volunteers of the community. Without the foresight and effort of many citizens, they would not exist, or certainly not as well. Many groups are responsible for their well-being.

Love of gardens, the past, and/or history may bring visitors to St. Mary's City. They may not have realized just what they would find there. However, the beauty and abundance of heritage found there will bring them back again and again.

FREEDOM RELEASED: FREEDOM OF CONSCIENCE GARDEN ▲
The Freedom of Conscience figure appears to be cleaving the stone from which it is emerging. The statue dominates the small garden around its base. Annuals surround the base while a new azalea garden is being developed behind the statue.

SUMMERTIME.: GARDEN OF REMEMBRANCE ◄
The Garden of Remembrance at St. Mary's College lies in the summer sun overlooking the river and sailboats below. Crepe myrtle provides summer color among the boxwood while the garden awaits the touch of frost to ignite the dogwood leaves and berries to flame.

MERRY FACES: MULBERRY SHOPPE HERB GARDEN ►
Shasta daisies lift their bright faces to the sun in the small herb garden of the Mulberry Shoppe.

CARDINAL DE RICHELIEU: OLD-FASHIONED ROSE GARDEN ▲
This gallica hybrid rose, a deep purple, is one of the beautiful flowers of the Old Fashioned Rose Garden of the Carroll County Farm Museum. The rose garden is one fourth of a larger set of historic gardens under development.

SMALL SUN: GREENWAY ARBORETUM ▶
Sitting in the desert garden among fellow residents of warm and dry habitat, this small cactus opens its golden blossom, its petals sheer as silk. Each plant within the desert house at Greenway Arboretum has interesting form and display as well as distinctive habitat.

HERB GARDEN: Stillridge Herb Garden

Paths to follow, leaves to taste, redolent odors to smell, and bees and butterflies to share the garden are all at Stillridge Herb Garden. If the single plants of the garden prove too few for the visitor's taste, he or she can go into the fields and see the herbs row on row.

TREASURE IN COLOR: NATIONAL COLONIAL FARM KITCHEN GARDEN
The Kitchen Garden is one of the gardens devoted to the collection and conservation of plants of heritage at the National Colonial Farm in Accokeek. Here the most humble vegetable is allowed to send its blossoms forth to set seed in the proper time.

NETTIE JONES GARDEN: THE GARDENS OF THE HISTORICAL SOCIETY OF TALBOT COUNTY
The Nettie Jones Garden is one of a trio of gardens at the Historical Society while the North Terrace Garden and the South Terrace Garden complete the set. Enclosed with brick wall and picket fence, each with designs reminiscent of historical ties at Wye Mills, the gardens are veritable touchstones of history.

NOTES AND DIRECTIONS

St. Mary's City Gardens

Hours: Daylight

Season: June through August

Services: Tours, lectures, luncheon, and gift shop.

Admission: Some with fee, some non-fee

Information: Note: A half-day minimum should be devoted to the area. A fee is required for some of the gardens and other attractions. Groups would be well-advised to call ahead of time to schedule their trip.

Phone: There are three governing bodies involved in the gardens in St. Mary's City. For information on the Garden of Remembrance and the St. Mary's College Herb Garden, call St. Mary's College Public Information Office (301) 862-0380. For the Mulberry Shoppe, call (301) 872-4293, and for all the remaining St. Mary's City gardens, call Historic St. Mary's City (301) 862-0990 or (301) 862-0960

Directions:

From Washington:

From the Washington Beltway, take Route 5 south to Waldorf. It will be joined for a while by Route 301. Continue on Route 5 until it turns off after Mechanicsville. At this point, the two-lane highway becomes Route 235. Take Route 235 south past Hollywood until reaching Lexington Park. Turn right on Route 246 to rejoin Route 5. On Route 5, turn south to St. Mary's City. Signs are visible directing the visitor to the Information Center. (If this digression from Route 5 and back to Route 5 seems a bit out of the way, a glance at a road map will show that Route 5 wanders considerably before arriving at St. Mary's City. The jog from one route to another is actually simpler if not shorter.)

From Baltimore:

From the Baltimore Beltway, take Exit 3 (Route 2 south) to Route 301. Continue to Marlboro where it intersects Route 4 and travel on Route 4 south (becomes Routes 2 and 4) to the end of Calvert County and cross the bridge into St. Mary's County. At Route 235, turn south and continue until reaching Lexington Park. Turn right on Route 246 to join Route 5. On Route 5, turn south to St. Mary's City. Signs are visible directing the visitor to the Information Center.

CHAPTER FIVE

Town and Country Living

In the past as in the present, living in the country had the benefits of clean air, few people, reduced traffic, and quiet. Some of the colonists enjoyed the country life as opposed to town life even though town was not much by the standards of today. This chapter on town and country life includes five gardens from the country and one set of town gardens. In the Carroll County Farm Museum Old-Fashioned Rose Garden, heritage roses join, without intention, other gardens across the state in preservation of heritage plant material. Also in Carroll County, but yet to make its mark in the plant world, the Greenway Arboretum is young indeed. With bright rolling hills amidst what was once farmland, it has a lot of living and growing to do to try to catch such patricians of the arbor world as the Cedar of Lebanon at Hampton National Historic Site or the Wye Oak in Talbot County. In lower Prince George's County, near Accokeek, the National Colonial Farm Kitchen Garden works with heritage seed plants and actively participates in the network across the nation in building up a seed bank of historic seeds. Growing plants with a heritage rather than

heritage plants, Stillridge Herb Farm is close enough to Baltimore to be within a 20-minute drive. Even so, it retains the feeling of country. The heritage of a way of life is held for posterity at the Sotterley Plantation. Finally, the gardens at the Historic Society of Easton, Maryland, are studded with the heritage of history. With these many gardens out in the country or small town, it is no wonder that Maryland is rich with gardening resources, for not only do Marylanders of the metropolis have access to beautiful and historical places, but her citizens of the countryside do also.

Carroll County Farm Museum's Old-Fashioned Rose Garden

Old-fashioned roses with their petals spread like skirts

The Old-Fashioned Rose Garden is part of a growing garden enclosed with a white picket fence on the Carroll Country Farm Museum grounds. The beautiful roses in this garden remind visitors that farmers and their wives love their gardens as much as any of their city-bred cousins. It is in the heart of

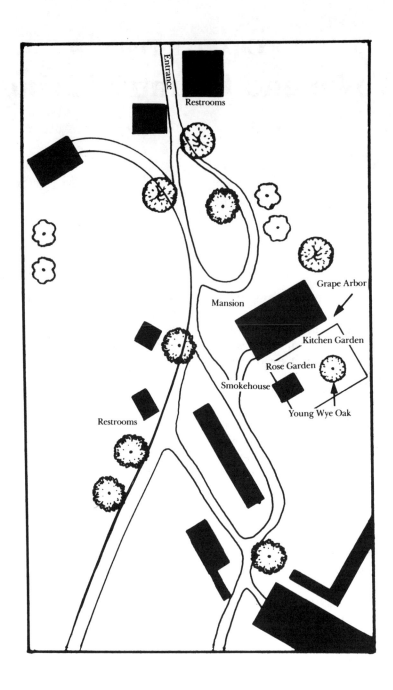

CARROLL COUNTY FARM MUSEUM / OLD-FASHIONED ROSE GARDEN

Old Fashioned Roses

Species Roses

Austrian Copper, *Rosafoetida bicolor*, pre-1590. Flower petals orange on upper side, yellow underneath. Origin, Asia; Father Hugo's Rose, *R. hugonis*, 1899. Discovered by a French priest in China. Early blooming, single yellow flowers; one of the few yellow roses; Sweet Brier, *R. eglanteria*, The wild rose of song and story, native to Europe. Foliage smells like apples. Located by the gazebo, June blooming.

French Roses (Gallic)

Apothecary Rose or Red Rose of Lancaster, *R. gallica officinalis*. An old rose grown by the Romans. Very fragrant, it is much used for perfume and potpourri. 28 petals; Rosa Mundi, *R. gallica versicolor*, pre-1580. Pale pink or white flowers are stripped with red, all different; Tuscany, sometimes called Old Velvet, *R. gallica hybrid*, pre-1596. Maroon-crimson flowers with golden centers; Cardinal de Richelieu, *R. gallica hybrid*, 1840. Fragrant, dark rose-purple flowers. Originally named Rose Van Sian.

White Roses (Alba)

White Rose of York, *R. alba maxima*, pre-1579. An ancient rose which became a symbol during the English War of Roses. Creamy white flowers followed by showy red fruits (hips); Konigin Von Danemark (Queen of Denmark), *R. alba hybrid*, 1826. Warm pink flowers, very double, very fragrant. Showy fruits.

Damask Roses (Damascena)

York and Lancaster, *R. damascena versicolor*, 1551. Petals are red or white, no two flowers alike. Commemorating the white rose adopted as the badge of York, the red of Lancaster during the War of Roses; Celsiana, *R. damascena hybrid*, pre 1750. Large, pale pink flowers with open center, born in clusters, fragrant, 4-5 feet; Mme. Hardy, *R. damascena hybrid*, 1832. Hybridized by M. Hardy who was a gardener in the Luxembourg Gardens in Paris. One of the best white roses.

Portland Roses (Developed from Damask roses, they are repeat bloomers with fragrant, double flowers).

Jacques Cartier, 1868. Large and full flowers, light pink, darker center. Very fragrant; Comte de Chambord, 1860. Full, flat flowers, pink tinged with lilac. Very fragrant.

Centifolia (The rose of 100 petals known and grown by the Greeks).

Crested Moss or Chapeau de Napoleon, *R. centifolia cristata*, circa 1820. Green calyx with crested edge looks like a three-cornered hat. Discovered in a convent in Fribourg; Salet, *R. Centifolia muscosa*, 1854. Pink, fragrant, repeat bloom.

China Roses (*Chinensis*)

Old Blush, *R. chinensis semperflorens*, pre 1750. Early pink flowers, repeat bloom; Mutabilis, *R. chinensis mutabilis*, pre-1896. Remarkable for the changing colors of its flowers, first yellow, then orange, red and finally crimson; Hermosa, *R. chinensis hybrid*, 1840. Most beautiful pink blossoms on a low bush, repeat bloom, vigorous.

Noisette (China hybrids)

Blush Noisette, *R. chinensis manetti* or *noisettiana*, 1817. This hybrid created by John Champney of Charleston, S.C., introduced by the Noisette brothers of Paris. Pale pink.

Bourbon (From the Isle of Bourbon in the Indian Ocean, hybrids of China roses).

Souvenir de La Malmaison, *R. chinensis borbonniana*, 1843. An excellent and popular rose named for the home of Josephine Bonaparte. Fragrant, pink flowers; La Reine Victoria, (Bourbon rose), 1872. Bright pink, well-cupped, fragrant flowers.

Hybrid Perpetuals (A combination of many species).

Stanwell, *R. spinosissima hybrid* 1838. Its fine foliage and prickly canes resemble Scotch roses; Paul Neyron, (Hybrid perpetual), 1859. Very large, fragrant rose-pink flowers, repeat bloom.

Climbers

Sombreuil, 1850. Originated in France, fragrant, creamy white flowers.

Hybrid Teas

La France, 1867. A historic rose, being one of the first Hybrid Teas, originating in France.

Maryland farmland that this garden of historic roses blooms in open sunshine.

Once the site of the county almshouse in Westminster, the house was the residence of the poor. The land was farmed from the late 1850s until 1965 when the county commissioners established the Carroll County Farm Museum to represent a vanishing way of life. Now the gardens lying to the back of the house contain a smokehouse. Currently, the spire of the smokehouse shelters the home of a bee-hive. Visitors can watch the bees as they go in and out of the smokehole on their way to and from the fragrant flowers in the garden.

Lush, sweetly scented flowers, full-blown roses gently open beside still firmly packed buds rich with color yet unrevealed. Their colors range from white to cream to yellow, soft pink to flaming red, salmon to burgundy in solid colors, stripes, specks, and spots.

The rose garden provides another link in a chain being forged across the state. The Old-Fashioned Rose Garden is part of an unplanned effort to save the plants of the past beyond the hybridization of the present to have their genetic resources in the pool of the future. Like the seed saver and seed bank programs elsewhere, these living museums guarantee that if the strengths held within these historic plants are needed, they will be available.

Unlike the hybrids of the present, these heritage roses were, and are, resistant to many diseases that cause modern gardeners so much pain. Yet they are often more fragrant than the modern varieties, and for those looking to rose plants for their rosehips, some of their varieties provide large fruit abundantly. The petals and fruits of the heritage roses were used for potpourri as well as jelly. Also rosehip jelly was a common sick-room gift in the colonial days; rosehips

contain high levels of vitamin C.

The Old-Fashioned Rose Garden is the first small quarter of plans for a larger garden. Within the white picket fence surrounding the total area are the rose garden, the beginnings of a kitchen garden, a perennial garden, and an historic shrub garden. The spring of 1987 saw the first section of the kitchen garden in bloom. Between the kitchen garden and the perennial garden grows a hemlock hedge with an archway. A Wye Oak stripling about 12 feet tall has already found good footing and open sky in which to grow and provide shade for the perennial garden.

While the farm is rustic, it is very accessible to all visitors. Some sections are not as easily accessible to wheelchair-bound visitors as others. However, the rose garden is not large and a walk runs along two sides of it while the center of the garden is grassy.

Currently a single season garden, the garden's prime time is early summer. The roses begin to bloom in May and reach their peak in June. With all of the other attractions at the Farm Museum, a visit to the Old-Fashioned Rose Garden is icing on an interesting day's outing. This is a good garden to combine with a visit to Greenway Arboretum.

Greenway Arboretum

Hills of peace and promise

The Greenway Arboretum in Carroll County, begun in 1978, is young as far as arboreta go, but has considerable progress to show for its few years. It represents a great deal of promise with plenty of room to grow. As with a number of the other gardens and arboreta in this book, the dream of an arboretum lived in the heart of one person. The dream of creating an arboretum began for Mr. Zeeger DeWilde as he grew up in Holland. As a horticulturist/arborist, he was on loan from Holland to Canada to assist with Expo 67. After a number of years working in Canada, he took out Canadian citizenship. From Canada to the United States was a very short move indeed. A new marriage, a new family, and the opportunity to buy land for his dream set the stage for Greenway. Beginning with 27 open acres, DeWilde was able to start with a clean slate and draw—and plant—to his heart's content. The arboretum now contains 40 families of trees and a selection of shrubs which are attractively placed across the acreage. The original farmland had few existing trees. Spread across rolling hills, the elevation difference adds to the collection of points of prominence and swales of solitude. The beginnings of the interest points have been well situated.

The visitor's walk begins at the Country Emporium and Gift Shop with the first stop at a series of greenhouses. The most important one to visit is the zerophytic (desert) house with its very interesting collection of desert plants. The walks lead forward from one display bed to another. The display beds are used as accents rather than as separate gardens.

Aside from the specimen trees in this arboretum, an orchard is accompanied by a red caboose named the "Orchard Express." On another path, a gazebo rest area sits amid the Perennial Walk. The beauty of the seasons is heralded by spring bulbs in blossom and is followed by perennial and annuals in a rainbow of color. Clumps of ageratum, sweet alyssum, and Johnny-jump-ups intermingle with red geraniums and blue delphiniums. Giant allium send their purple balls of blossoms to stand high over shorter companions. All of these beds provide attractive islands urging the visitor forward to the next colorful spot.

This is a garden to grow with. It is not ready-made and will be many years in the growing. Being relatively close, it is well worth the visit in combination with a visit to the Carroll County Rose Garden. For those who live in the vicinity, it will be a source of repeated pleasure.

National Colonial Farm Kitchen Garden

An Heirloom Garden

After leaving the approach to Accokeek on Bryan Point Road in southern Prince George's County, the road is narrow and winding. It wanders along up hill and down until it arrives at the Saylor Memorial Grove parking lot for the National Colonial Farm. Alighting from the car, the visitor proceeds on foot, enjoying the quiet, country air and following a dirt road winding along between a pair of snake or split rail fences. Looking at the rails zigging and zagging back and forth along the way, held in place by stacks of posts, the wonder is that they do not fall down.

The visitor arrives at a kitchen garden of striking beauty, serving a surprising function. It is a living heirloom, providing seeds for posterity. The kitchen garden is part of the National Colonial Farm that has been conducting research projects for the Accokeek Foundation since 1958.

The garden is surrounded by a fence laced at the bottom half to deter small animals and entered by a rustic gate fastened with a wood latch. It is laid out in a group of raised beds retained by logs much as gardeners of today use railroad ties. This gives the garden a tidy appearance and allows visitors to walk through it without damaging the plants. Next to the garden is the outdoor kitchen complete with hearth, table, tools, and pot-

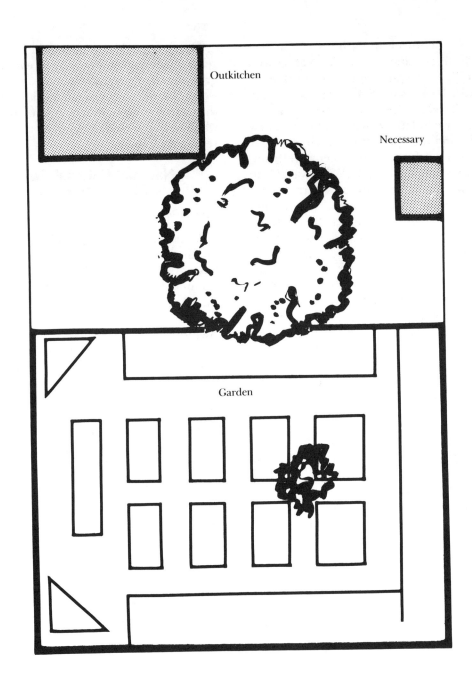

NATIONAL COLONIAL FARM KITCHEN GARDEN

tery; dried vegetables and herbs hang from the rafters below the ceiling.

The garden is not only beautiful in its rustic setting, but also serves as a source of seeds to add to those growing in other gardens as part of a seed saver service to keep viable those varieties that have fallen out of favor with the commercial seed companies. These varieties might otherwise be lost forever to the gardeners of the world.

Seeds for this garden have come from the National Small Grains Collection, U. S. Department of Agriculture, Beltsville, Maryland; seed savers in Missouri; and through the breeding and selection program at the farm. They have increased from a small handful of seed to enough to plant small fields. Spinach, beets, wheat, tobacco, and herbs are carefully nurtured through the full cycle of their life to maturity and fruition in order that their seeds can be gathered and saved for sharing and growing. After harvest they are transported to the climatically controlled seed storage room where they can be maintained for up to four years. Sharing through the Seed Savers Exchange not only allows other gardeners the opportunity to grow these historically important plants, but also increases the amount of seeds available through seed banks.

An arboretum of native Maryland trees will be the next step in the development of displays and in the preservation of plants at the farm. In the fall of 1987, plantings will begin for approximately 100 species of native trees. This will be the only arboretum in the state devoted to native trees.

The Kitchen Garden at the National Colonial Farm is a step back in time to living history. It may not be for everyone because of the rustic nature, but it is well worth seeing. Weekend demonstrations there include a variety of activities. Planting, seed collection, and storage are especially interesting. Visitors should call for information.

Stillridge Herb Farm and Garden

Harvest time with shears and basket

In a very rural setting open to the sunshine and filled with the peace and quiet of the country, Stillridge Herb Garden has been a source of abundance for its owner since 1970. It is far enough out in the country for one to feel that it is beyond city habitation, but near enough to the arteries of Baltimore to be within 20 minutes of downtown.

An herb garden, farm, and still room now constitute Stillridge. A commercial farm and garden owned by Mary Lou Riddle, Stillridge is open to the public for visits and tours of the garden and fields. Demonstrations and classes are held in the still room where the visitor quickly understands the name. Herbs hang or lie very quietly as the still, hot, and dry air removes the moisture from them, rendering them crisp and ready for packing into containers or for use in arrangements.

Row upon row of herbs of many different kinds spreads out over the fields. Nearer to the still room and house, herbs are planted in a garden more decoratively along walks and around ceramic pieces.

Visitors will find Rosemary for remembrance, once carried by brides at their weddings. Supposedly, it quickens the spirit and makes one more lively. Thyme, the symbol of courage and bravery, has been cultivated since the days of ancient Greece. Grown here in a number of different varieties, some are very aromatic while others are not. It is an essential herb for cooks. Sweet Marjoram, a symbol of happiness, was said to banish grief and bless the dead. Superstition caused it to be used in love potions and young lovers were crowned with it. Many more herbs are found here that invite bees and butterflies to sip and visitors to touch, taste, and smell their many qualities.

From June on, the visitor may watch harvesters with scissors in hand, snipping herbs and carefully laying them into baskets to be carried into the still room where they can dry without shattering. In the drying shed, the plant material is hung in bunches or laid on sheets of paper on boxes to dry. Moisture, the bane of the herbalist, is easy enough to avoid while drying plant material. The still room is kept hot by the summer sun and closed away from moist air. Moisture will make the flowers turn black and mildew grow on the stems.

Stillridge is a working herb garden. The plants that are grown in the garden provide seeds for those who wish to grow them. Plant materials are used for craft classes and for the bouquet, wedding, and other artistic arrangements sold in their shops. Visitors may also have luncheons seasoned with herbs and accompanied by herb beverages. Arrangements for luncheons need to be made ahead of time.

Walking about in the gardens and/or the drying shed is a very slow process as there is so much to see. A warm welcome is assured and repeat visits will be as refreshing as the first.

Sotterley Mansion Gardens

A tableland garden complete with candles

Deep in the heart of St. Mary's County lies the remnants of a stately southern plantation which dates back to the 1700s. The Sotterley Mansion and grounds remain a heritage from eight generations of ownership. Now under the Sotterley Mansion Foundation stewardship, it stands in proud memory of its past.

By their very nature, gardens appropriate to a plantation must be large. The Sotterley Gardens are indeed large, varied, and beautiful. Spread out on a tableland overlooking fields and river, and visible from the North Porch of the Mansion, the gardens feature in separate sections herbs, produce, and fruits for the kitchen as well as flowers for the tables. These gardens are representative of the large gardens that provided for a plantation's needs.

The two acres of gardens are laid out in a rectangle divided into four parts with paths crossing off-center in both directions. While the vegetable and herb gardens once fed the entire plantation's residents, it now provides the basis for jams, preserves, and other delicacies sold in the Gift Shop. The flower garden still provides bouquets for the house.

Bloom time for Sotterley is from the earliest spring to the latest fall with color at all times. Mid-May is special for its display of peonies. During the summer the gardens are a riot of color. Iris beds are extensive and roses are followed by yucca blossoms, glistening white "Candles of the Lord," which stand heads above the lower plants. A butterfly weed glows warmly in the sun. Between the gardens grass lawn provides walkways. There are no steps or stairs in the garden.

A sundial of English make, from about 1925, stands on the orchard side. Made of slate, it stands on a pedestal which bears the Plater, Briscoe, and Satterlee coats-of-arms bearing testimony to the families who have lived at Sotterley. If the similarity of names, Sotterley and Satterlee, seems confusing or perhaps a problem of misspelling, it is no wonder. Sotterley plantation's first name in 1659 was Resurrection Manor; it was owned by Thomas Cornwallis. The house which has been known as Sotterley was built in the early years of the 1700s. After his death the property changed hands within the family resulting in the Plater period from 1729 to 1822. With a turn of the dice, according to tradition, Sotterley was lost. The Briscoe family, Emeline and Dr. Walter Hanson Stone Briscoe, was the next to live at Sotterley from 1822 to 1910. Finally in 1910 Herbert Satterlee bought Sotterley.

Because both the Sotterley Mansion Gardens and the gardens in St. Mary's City are in St. Mary's County and entail a lengthy drive for most visitors, they could be combined to make a full day's excursion. It is advisable to call ahead to the gardens involved and make arrangements.

The Gardens of the Historical Society of Talbot County

Touched with history

A touchstone of history has been provided in the gardens behind the Historical Society of Talbot County's buildings in Easton, Maryland. Designed in the style of the 17th century Federal period, three gardens flow around, between, and behind the buildings in an irregular pattern, approximately 100 by 300 feet. The North Terrace Garden and the South Terrace Garden are on Washington Street, but they are entered from the interior of the garden complex. The North Terrace Garden lies between the Historical Society's building and an old store building owned by the society to preserve the continuity of the area. The South Terrace Garden, currently being given a face-lift, is at the corner of Washington Street and Glenwood Avenue. The Nettie Jones Garden to the rear of the South Terrace Garden is the third garden. Over 30 years of labor and love have been devoted to the creation of these gardens by members of both the Historical Society and the Talbot County Garden Club.

Befitting its connection to the Historical Society, there are garden components that are historical and others that are representative or evocative of historical sites in the county, state, or young nation. The bricks in the walks and walls are a century old. The bricks in the herringbone patterned walks and terrace of the North Terrace Garden came from the sidewalks of early Easton. A beautiful wrought iron gate at the entrance to the North Terrace Garden originated in Charleston. On the north wall of the North Terrace Garden a stone lion-head stands ready to spew forth water into the basins of a wall fountain. The picket fence and gate, which approach and embrace two enormous sycamore trees at the Glenwood Avenue entrance, are styled after the fence at the 18th century Chase Lloyd House in Annapolis.

Wye Mills was important in Talbot County and has had an influence in the Talbot County Historic Society's gardens. Within the gardens of the Historic Society, the Wye House and the famous Wye Oak are represented in two ways. First, the style of the brick wall which runs along two sides is taken from that of the wall at the cemetery of the Wye House. Second, the acorn finials for the picket fence are shaped like the acorns of the Wye Oak.

The plants within the garden are in keeping with those that would have been planted in the Federal period, including crepe myrtle, historic roses, *Vinca minor*, ivy, camellias, spring bulbs, dogwood, and boxwood. Walks and beds are surrounded with strips of lawn. Fruit trees, typical of such gardens, are planted along with 100 small boxwood that line a 20-foot-wide grand walk. Another 100 boxwood were used to enhance the garden.

Shady in part, these gardens are best seen in their most colorful attire in June. Access is relatively easy. The brick walks may be uneven in places because of the growth of trees and the space between the beds is often lawn. Altogether, these gardens are very nice indeed.

Notes and Directions

Carroll County Farm Museum Rose Garden

Hours: M - F, 10 a.m. - 4 p.m.; Sat., Sun., 12 noon - 5 p.m.

Season: May-June

Services: Tours

Admission: Fee

Information: Open late May to end of October on weekends. Open every day during July and August. Special rates for large groups. Ideal for school groups. Call for group visits of 20 or more. Fair access to wheelchair-bound visitors.

Phone: (301) 848-7775 or (301) 876-2667

Directions:
From Westminster:

Take Route 140 to Center Street. Turn south on Center Street. Cross Main Street and Green Street. Follow Center Street bearing left and then right. Turn in at the sign for the Carroll County Farm Museum at 500 Center Street.

Greenway Gardens and Arboretum

Hours: M - Sat., 9 a.m. - 5 p.m.; Sun., noon - 5 p.m.; open late till 9 p.m. on Thur.

Season: Spring through fall (open year round)

Services: Classes, group outings, tours, and gift shop

Admission: Fee

Information: While lengthy, the walks are free of obstructions to the handicapped. Like most arboreta, however, the area is large and the visitor should expect a good deal of exercise. Educational programs and gifts are available in the gift shop. A picnic area is also available to visitors. Calling for information on the availability of the arboretum and other areas to groups would be a good idea, particularly if the visit is combined with a visit to another garden.

Phone: (301) 876-3213

Directions:
From Westminster:

Go south on Route 97, pass Route 32 to Nicodemus Road. Turn left on Nicodemus Road. After 9.0 miles, look for Greenway on the left. If you arrive once more at Route 32, you have missed it. Note: Nicodemus Road is fragmented and it is possible to be on a section of it and not find what you are looking for. You need the small portion which lies between Routes 97 and 32.

National Colonial Farm Kitchen Garden

Hours: T - Sun., 10 a.m. - 5 p.m. Closed Mondays, Thanksgiving, Christmas, and New Year's Day.

Season: June through September

Services: Tours, lectures, demonstrations

Admission: Fee (Children under 12 free)

Information: Groups should make prior arrangements. Handicapped Access: The Accokeek Foundation and the National Park Service have attempted to provide the necessary steps to allow all people to visit and enjoy the National Colonial Farm. The National Colonial Farm staff has been trained to assist impaired visitors. A vehicle for physically handicapped individuals is available by pre-arrangement. For further information or assistance, please call (301) 283-2113. The walkways within the garden are bark.

Phone: (301) 283-2115

Directions:

From Washington:

Take the Beltway (I-95) to exit 3. (Stay in the right lane). Go south on Indian Head Highway (Route 210) for 9.4 miles to Bryan Point Road fork, south of Fort Washington in Accokeek, MD.

Note: The intersection was revised in 1987. About 0.25 mile prior to the intersection, a service road from Route 210 to the right is marked "To Bryan Point Road." This information may not be on the map followed by the visitor.

Take Bryan Point Road 3.8 miles to the farm entrance at Saylor Memorial Grove parking area. The road is well-marked with brown rectangular signs.

Stillridge Herb Farm and Garden

Hours: M - Sat., 9 a.m - 4 p.m.

Season: June through September

Services: Classes, tours, lectures, gift shop, luncheons by prior arrangement.

Admission: None

Information: The garden is open to visitors; tours and luncheons must have prior arrangements. A working garden, it is not designed for the handicapped.

Phone: (301) 465-8348

Directions:

From Baltimore:

Take Route 40 west or Route 70 west to Route 29. Turn north to Route 99. Turn left (west) on Route 99 and continue for 3 miles.

A sign for Stillridge will be on the right. A small drive will lead back to the Stillridge Herb Farm.

From Columbia/Washington:

Take Route 29 north to Route 99. Turn west for 3 miles. A sign for Stillridge will be on the right. A small drive will lead back to the Stillridge Herb Farm: 10370 Route 99, Woodstock, MD 21163. Do not be misled by the Woodstock address. Stillridge is situated between Ellicott City and Woodstock in Howard County.

Sotterley Plantation Gardens

Hours: M - Sun., 11 a.m. - 5 p.m.; Daily June 1 - September 30

Season: Spring through September

Services: Tours, gift shop, transportation from the boat dock to the mansion.

Admission: Fee

Information: It may be visited April, May, October, and November by appointment. Luncheon for groups may be arranged. Parties are welcome to bring lunches. It is moderately accessible for the handicapped, but not recommended for the wheelchair-bound.

Phone: (301) 373-2280

Directions:

By Car

From Baltimore:

From the Baltimore Beltway, take Route 301 south to Waldorf. Make a left turn at the traffic light on Route 5 until it turns off after Mechanicsville. At this point, the two-lane highway becomes Route 235. Take Route 235 south to Hollywood, make a left turn on Route 245, and proceed 3 miles to Sotterley on the right.

From Washington:

From the Washington Beltway, take Route 5 south to Waldorf. It will be joined for a while by Route 301. Continue on Route 5 until it turns off after Mechanicsville. At this point, the two-lane highway becomes Route 235. Take Route 235 south to Hollywood, make a left turn onto Route 245, and proceed 3 miles to Sotterley on the right.

By Boat:

The Sotterley Mansion dock on the Patuxent River provides docking for deep draft boats and transportation from the dock to the gardens.

The Gardens of the Historic Society of Talbot County

Hours: The gardens are never closed, but the office and museum for the Historical Society are open T-Sat., 10 a.m.-4 p.m., Sun., 10 a.m.-4 p.m. in summer.

Season: Spring through fall

Services: Tours available

Admission: None

Information: Relatively accessible to the handicapped. Brick walks and lawn separate the beds; steps are encountered in moving from the lower garden to the North Terrace Garden or to the South Terrace Garden. The two terrace gardens are separated by a building owned by the Historic Society. Call for information or tour planning.

Phone: (301) 822-0733

Directions:

From Easton in Talbot County:

The center of town may be approached from the Easton bypass by (Route 322) via either Route 333 or Route 33 to Washington Street. Proceed on Washington Street to Glenmont Avenue. Parking is available in a parking alley between Glenmont Avenue and Dover Street. The parking alley runs along the back side of the gardens and to the side of the Historic Society's building. The garden entrance is on Glenmont Avenue just off Washington Street in the heart of Easton. A white picket fence and gate will grant admittance. Feed the parking meters; ticketing is enforced!

CHAPTER SIX
Specialties

Gardens that specialize in a particular plant group or style of plant treatment may be single season gardens or gardens that are nice to see most of the growing season. Of the six included in this chapter, two are single season gardens; one is devoted to plants referred to in the Bible; one has a broad spectrum of water plants; one specializes in attracting, caring for, and feeding butterflies; and the last is a living heritage of topiary.

The two single season gardens, Brighton Dam and McCrillis, are azalea gardens. Stylewise, the azalea gardens are very different. Brighton Dam Azalea Garden was planted in block fashion in order to get a mass effect. When in bloom, it is a veritable patchwork carpet of color. McCrillis Garden is more spacious, if not as large. The paths are placed so that varieties may be seen as individuals giving the visitor a good view of what a specific plant looks like and also a feeling of openness and air.

Ladew Topiary Gardens in Harford County are more park-like or dress-up gardens. There is the feeling that at any moment the visitor might see ladies in billowing skirts drift into sight as the queen's court of *Alice in Wonderland* appears. The Ladew Topiary Gardens are very nearly all-year gardens. The flower beds are beautiful during the growing season, but many of the topiary pieces are evergreen, beautiful before the flowers arrive and long after they are gone.

The Christ Church Biblical Garden of Port Republic in Calvert County is most beautiful in the spring, but has merit through the summer. Christ Church Biblical Garden is a small retreat for a private visit, a stop by the wayside for the weary and a treasure for the gardener.

Lilypons, south of Fredrick, with its many kinds of water plants and the added attraction of water fowl and koi (Japanese carp) is an all-season garden. This garden is for the patient seeker. This is a working country garden open to the elements. It is broad spread and inset with a myriad of glistening pools planted with water lilies and visited by their many feathered friends basking in the sunlight.

The Prince George's Butterfly Garden is best seen (especially by the visitor coming from a distance) in mid-to late summer when the population of butterflies is at its peak. The Butterfly Garden is in the Cosca Regional Park near Clinton in Prince George's County.

Brighton Dam Azalea Garden

One man's dream realized

It is the dream of men to make a mark in the world that will be noted long after the fact of its accomplishment. The azalea garden at Brighton Dam is surely a dream come true and has certainly been noticed long after its inception.

The dream belonged to Raymond W. Bellamy, a former chairman of the Washington Suburban Sanitary Commission. It was his dream to see the shorelines of the Tridelphia reservoir planted with azaleas. The dream at Brighton Dam is a 22,000-azalea reality.

Those original azaleas, and the ones that followed, survived and thrived. Currently, they provide a living wall of color close at hand or a colorful carpet beneath the trees when viewed from a distance. Glenn Dale, Kurume, Indicas, Macrantha, Joseph Gable, and Mollis are among the azalea varieties that reside in the five major divisions of the garden.

The topography is one of rolling hills with folds and gentle slopes. A circular observation site allows a raised view of the gardens. Plans for the future include a raised observation tower to be built upon this site. A gravel drive winds in, around, and through the mass of color. From a distance, the effect is that of a woodland with a flowing carpet of blazing irregular design. It is hard to decide which is the most advantageous point of view, standing within the garden or sitting off-shore looking in. Looking out across the lake, one can see azalea beds on other slopes, glowing beneath the spring green-tipped

trees and reflected in the water. With over 8,000 visitors going through the garden over the weekend during its peak season, there is no claiming that it is overlooked. During April and May, this floral rainbow garden receives visitors from across the nation.

The 1986 season opened with a new addition for the elderly and the handicapped. Drivers with handicapped or elderly passengers are permitted to drive through the garden during the week. During the weekends, though, there are too many visitors to allow cars; however, a new golf cart is now available for special visitors to be escorted through the grounds.

The Kurume Azaleas kick off the spring season. There are seven varieties at Brighton from the shell pink of Coral Bells to the scarlet of Hinodgiri. The most compact grower of the group is Snow, pure white.

Midseason bloom is provided by Joseph Gable, the Mollis varieties, and Indica Rosea. The Joseph Gable and Mollis are both hybrid groups. Herbert and Royalty (Joseph Gable) provide deep colors, Herbert with large frilled and ruffled flowers and Royalty with double flowers of bright purple.

Mollis hybrids are unusual because they are deciduous. Their blossoms leave the usual pink to red spectrum and present beautiful yellow and orange to orange-red colors. The plants are upright, tall and neat of habit.

Glacier (Glenn Dale) is another midseason azalea with large growth and white blossoms. Another Glenn Dale, Salmon Queen, picks up the time line as a very late bloomer. It is a very large plant with salmon colored blossoms. Joining with Salmon Queen at the end of the season are Indica Magnifica (spotted and flushed pink), Indica Alba (white), and Macrantha (salmon red and very late).

The visitor's timing is important for this single season garden for it is not open during

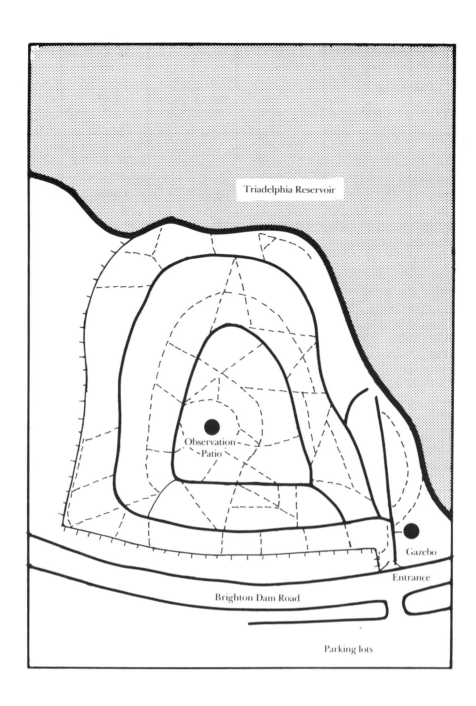

BRIGHTON DAM AZALEA GARDEN

the rest of the year. With the crush of visitors on the weekend, it is best enjoyed during a midweek morning.

Christ Church Biblical Garden

Consider the lilies of the field . . .

The Biblical Garden at Christ Church is laid out as two outdoor rooms built side by side, one entering from the outside and the other from the first. A meandering walk moves through the first, or the anteroom, to the quiet or contemplative garden which lies within a rosy brick wall. Implanted in the wall dividing the Biblical Garden from the Quiet Garden is a stone sundial. Unlike its horizontal counterparts, this sundial is vertical. Small scooped-out hollows catch the light and count the hours. Within the confines of both gardens grow shrubs, herbs, and bulbs whose commonality is their reference in scripture. (Only Biblical plants are planted in both gardens.)

With all of its numbers of plants of differing needs, the Biblical Garden at Christ Church has a well-loved look to it. Small gardens require a lot of constant attention to present a well-defined appearance. While the plantings are close, the care which they have been given allows the viewer to see the individual specimens.

Plants cited in scripture did not originate in this country; therefore, not all of those cited in the Bible are present in this garden. In some cases, different varieties have been tried to find the variety that would do well in Maryland weather and soil. A few have to live in pots so that they may be sheltered through the winter to survive.

The Quiet Garden is divided into four sections by a walk laid down in the shape of a cross. Centered at the junction of the arms of the "crosswalk" stands a wooden cross with figures of Adam and Eve carved in the center. As a contemplative garden, the Quiet Garden has benches with a water fountain set in the wall at the base of the crosswalk. Planted in a more formal arrangement with boxwood surrounds, tamarisk along one wall, and a fig tree in one corner, the Quiet Garden lends itself to peace and contemplation. A white rose climbs the separating wall, lending grace and a delightful scent.

Although small, the garden provides beauty and food for thought. Certainly a would-be biblical scholar could find an abundance of subjects to study in this garden. An absence of steps, access to rest rooms, and a cool drink of water allow everyone a feeling of welcome. The garden is small enough that a trip to see only this garden might not be worth the distance. However, for those who are interested, there are additional attractions within the church. Behind and to the side of the church lies a cemetery with interesting headstones and small iron fence-enclosed plots which would certainly round out the trip.

Ladew Topiary Gardens

Topiary . . . the art of training, cutting, or trimming plants and trees into fanciful shapes

The first visit to Ladew Topiary Gardens promotes a feeling that, like Alice, a fall into a rabbit hole has ended in Wonderland. The door to Maryland's Wonderland is in Harford County north of Baltimore. Within Ladew, trees look like walls and shrubs look like lyrebirds, chess pieces, squirrels, or other animals. Fourteen acres of magic can be wandered in all. The hunt scene complete with fox, hounds, and hunter, dressed in their healthy green leaves, flows across the first lawn as the visitor walks along the drive. This is a taste of the visual pleasures which await

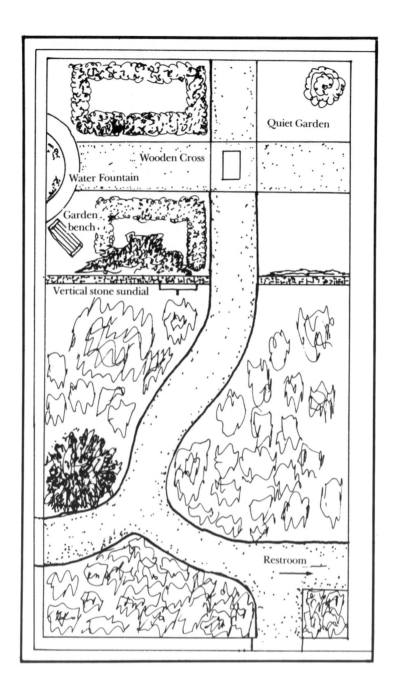

Quiet Garden

Wooden Cross

Water Fountain

Garden
bench

Vertical stone sundial

Restroom

CHRIST CHURCH BIBLICAL GARDEN

Plants and Their Biblical Reference

Almond	Genesis 30:37
Anemone	Matthew 6: 28-30
Anthemis	Song of Solomon 2:1-2
Apricot	Genesis 30:37
Artemisia	Duteronomy 29:18
Bay	Psalms 37:35
Boxwood	Isaiah 41:19
Cedar	Numbers 19:1,2,6
Chicory	Exodus 12:8
Crocus	Song of Solomon 6:4
Endive	Exodus 12:8
Fig	Genesis 3:7
Glastonbury Thorn	Mathew 7:15,16,17,20
Grapes	Genesis 9:20,21
Heath	Jeremiah 17:6
Ivy	II Maccabees 6:7
Juniper	Kings 19:5, Jeremiah 17:6
Leeks	Numbers 11:15
Love-in-a-mist/*Nigella sativa*	Isaiah 28:23,24,25,26,27
Madonna Lilies	Song of Solomon 6:2
Mint	Matthew 23:23
Mustard	Matthew 13:31-32
Narcissus	Isaiah 35:1
Oleaster	Isaiah 41:19
Onions	Numbers 11:5
Pine	II Samuel 6:5
Pomegranate	Exodus 28:33-34
Poppies	Matthew 6:28-30
Redbud	Matthew 27:5
Rue	Luke 11:42
Saffron	Song of Solomon 4:14
Sage	Exodus 37:17-18
Star of Bethlehem	II Kings 6:25
Sternbergia	Song of Solomon 2:1-2
Storay	Ecclesiasties 29:15
Tamarisk	Genesis 21:15, 33
Yellow Iris	Hosea 14:5

(For a complete work on plants of the of the Bible, see *All The Plants of the Bible* by Winifred Walker, Doubleday and Company, Inc., Garden City, N.Y., 1979) beyond the Ladew house.

Harvey Smith Ladew, a golden child born in 1886 with a gold spoon in his mouth, never knew the trials most mortals experience. His philosophy was never to be under the weather; there were so many other places to go. The Ladew House exhibits his joy of life.

If the collections of furnishings and room design within the house reflect one side of the joyous Harvey Ladew, the gardens certainly reflect the other. His plans for the development of the gardens ran far beyond his lifetime. Even so, his topiary gardens exceeded the efforts of all other individuals in America.

While the garden grows from the elegance of the 1800s, it is in keeping with Mr. Ladew's style that the garden is not limited and is fashioned in the style of the moment as he saw it. As he planned special rooms with unusual design in the house, he also exhibited the same flair in the trimming of the topiary and the implementation of *color* gardens. There are gardens with single color plantings of white, red, pink, and yellow.

Mr. Ladew made many changes to the gardens and the topiary pieces in his time. For instance, the design of the trimming varied from year to year. One year it was trimmed one way and years later another. Fortunately for today's staff, he had a passion for photographs and scrapbooks. It is possible to see that the trimming of a given piece varied from year to year.

When Harvey Ladew began his garden in 1929, he determined to do it himself. If he was not knowledgeable about landscaping and gardening, he would learn. He wanted to make his own mistakes and profit from them. He admitted to making them and to learning from them, giving credit to his mistakes for his accumulation of experience. In 1971, 42 years after the gardens began, he

was awarded the Distinguished Service Medal of the Garden Club of America for his great interest in developing and maintaining the most outstanding topiary garden in America without professional help. He was very proud of that award. He bequeathed the gardens and the manor house for the educational and cultural enrichment of the public, and he set up the foundation that supervises both.

Passing the house, the visitor is led from one doorway to another across 14 acres looking into garden room after garden room or hall. The pink garden, the white garden, the rose garden, the yellow garden, the iris garden, and the topiary are everywhere. Topiary pieces stand sentinel at entryways, sit in assemblage in their own garden, or provide decorated walls for the rooms and halls of the gardens.

Archways, gates, and paths, as well as steps and stairs, lead from one garden to another. Ornamental pools with ornate, formal shapes reflect the sky and garden around them. A guided stream flows through the iris garden into a pool in the middle of which a green Chinese junk sets its red sails into the wind. Close by, a green Buddha sits in silent meditation.

Crested, fluffy-tailed cockatoos sit in guardian splendor on either side of the entrance from the house to the amphitheater, the Great Bowl. A large green oval expanse, enclosing a pool and enclosed by walls trimmed with swags on one side and waves and swans on the opposite, is the scene of evening concerts.

The gardens have plants flowering in succession making repeat visits far from boring. The iris garden may exhibit Bearded Iris on one visit and Japanese Iris and day lilies on another. Trees and shrubs join in the merry-go-color as the green-on-green of summer

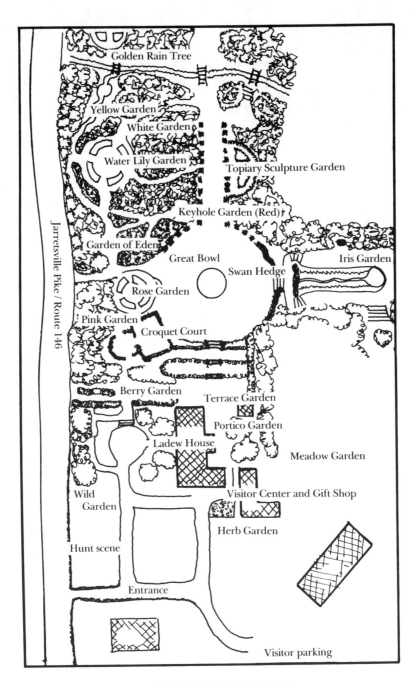

LADEW TOPIARY GARDENS

turns into a green-on-color tapestry for fall. With this kaleidoscope of flowers and color ever-changing, it is no wonder that repeat visitors often choose to take out membership in the Ladew Topiary Gardens Foundation so they may return again and again.

It is not possible to please all of the people at the same time, but the gardens at Ladew surely ought to please most of the people any time they visit. A topiary purist might make a face at the flower gardens intermixed with the topiary pieces, while the flower enthusiast might decide that the gardens will be prettier when they have more flowers. The visitor who goes to enjoy what the day and the gardens have to offer will find immeasurable delights.

Lilypons Water Gardens

A working garden with a popular attraction

Begun in 1925, the Lilypons Water Gardens were graced on their naming day by the presence of a Metropolitan Opera star by the same name, Lily Pons. Celebrating its 50th year in 1986, Lilypons had a reenactment of that day of dedication. Although many customers come to buy water lilies and other water garden supplies, the garden is also open to visitors. Three hundred acres lying along riverside have ample water supply for the five hundred ponds of Lilypons Water Gardens. There is plenty of room for two sets of visitors: visitors who come to see the water lilies and those who come to see the water birds. The dikes which separate the ponds provide a wide footpath where employees and visitors find comfortable, if not paved, walking.

This is a rough garden to be sure, but for those who enjoy open space, few people, beautiful flowers, birds, and clean air, it is hard to match. It does generate mixed reactions in visitors, however. The beauty of the catalog for Lilypons creates a sense of expectation of perfect beauty in the gardens themselves. Beauty is there, but not in layout or design.

In the morning light, an early visitor arrived at Lilypons Gardens dressed in a neat grey suit and with a quiet, serious mien. Two even earlier arrivals began to stalk him, also serious in their intent to lay claim to his attention. As they approached with cautious stealth, first one and then another would stop, make gestures and noises, and then begin their slow approach once more. With dignity, the Great Blue Heron allowed the photographers to approach within 15 feet. He was not disturbed by their clicking cameras. They in turn, having gotten their fill, were content to withdraw without having disturbed his contemplative review of the pond before him in his search for breakfast.

Canada geese can be heard chattering amongst themselves as they circle about above. A Great White Heron can be seen gliding across the ponds in the distance. Clearly, Lilypons has an attraction for both birds and bird-watchers as well as those who stalk the water lily. There are very few gardens where the visitor can watch as Canada geese come sailing in with their wings and feet bracing to land a short distance away, see them with their fluffy yellow/black goslings walking around, or watch egrets poised intently waiting for lunch.

One delightful thing about the garden is the accidental inclusion of wild plants that, representing a working burden to the employees to keep them in control, add to the birds' enjoyment and display beauty themselves. If the lily ponds provide food for the waterfowl, sunflowers and thistle invite the seed-eating birds to lunch.

As with most gardens, return visits are fresh and new for there is a succession of bloom in the water lilies matching that of any other type of garden. The bloom succession goes around the day as well as across the summer. For the visitor who has a single mental image of white or yellow water lilies, there is the surprise of seeing delicate pink, shocking magenta, sky blue, or deep blue blossoms. Lotus blossoms shimmer in glowing pink, white with tips of pink, gleaming white, or lemon yellow. A very early morning visit permits the sight of night-blooming varieties.

Along with colorful flowers and pond plants, the gardens provide koi (Japanese carp) to lend colorful form and movement in the pond water below. An amusing story is told about the koi. At one time the beautiful fish at Lilypons were in unrestricted ponds. As happens with rivers, there was a flood. The waters came up over the gardens, releasing the koi from their small pools. The employees at Lilypons speculate that there were some very surprised fishermen downstream.

Two festivals are celebrated annually at Lilypons: the Lotus Blossom Festival and the Koi Festival. The dates of the festivals are variable. The expectant visitor should call early in the spring to ascertain each date. During these festivals public restrooms are brought in and there are facilities for the handicapped. Other than these occasions, restroom facilities are on the second floor of the office building and are not readily accessible. Future plans include some landscaping with formal ponds, lending a visual demonstration to visitors on suggestions for using lily ponds in a site of their own choosing.

Visitors are welcomed, assisted when desired, otherwise left alone to enjoy the gardens and the birds. The day begins early at Lilypons so the visitor may also arrive with the cool of the morning and the breakfast-seeking birds.

McCrillis Gardens and Gallery

Line and form in plant and art

William McCrillis, Assistant to the Secretary of the Interior during the administration of three United States Presidents, collected azaleas and had an impressive array when he and his wife, Virginia, donated their house and five acres of wooded, shady, gardens to the Maryland National Capital Park and Planning Commission in 1987.

Just inside the Washington Beltway, McCrillis is located in the northern residential community of Bethesda. Managed by Brookside Gardens, the McCrillis Gardens continue to be refined into a beautiful shade garden. Ultimately, it will have a display period extending across most of the growing season. Prime bloom times for the rhododendrons and azaleas will not be changed, but the pleasure of the garden will be enhanced.

Its location within the residential section presents its only drawback in that parking is limited to a nearby school parking lot after school time and on weekends. Senior citizens and the handicapped, however, may be discharged within the circular driveway.

McCrillis is definitely the garden to see for those who wish to grow azaleas. In addition to the many older varieties, there are test plots containing 300 varieties of Satsuki (satski) imported from Japan and expected on the market in the late 1980s or early 1990s. Very late bloomers, the Satsuki will extend the gardener's azalea blooming season into June. In the case of the older varieties of azaleas, a number are no longer on the market. McCrillis now serves as a repository of these beautiful plants.

Aside from the aesthetics of the plantings,

the spacing of the plants allows the visitor to see the form of the plant. One of the most striking azaleas is Koromo Shikibu (listed as a Krume), a delightful lavender blossom with spider-like petals and upthrusting anthers. It is seen in both a loose growth and a more compact shrub. Attractive both ways, the more compact flowering seems to emphasize the detail of the floral bloom.

Early morning light slipping through the branches of the tree canopy over the gardens touches off a veritable rainbow of color as it moves. Wide bark-covered paths and well-spaced plantings give the gardens openness, allowing plants to be seen individually as well as in groupings.

McCrillis is a single season garden to be sure, but with over 750 varieties, the range of blooming season extends from mid-March until the end of June. Other plants acting as accent plants set off the central figures; daffodils, tulips, ferns, and jack-in-the-pulpit add to the spring look.

With beauty of mass color, it is easy to forget that the form of the mature plant is part of its attraction. Attention given to the space mature specimens need and ongoing care prevent plants from becoming clogged with dead and/or misshapen branches. This practice has prevented the garden from growing old, in spite of the fact that it can count more than 45 years since its beginning.

The McCrillis house is attractively set with azaleas and with tulips and other spring bulbs. Now serving as an art gallery, it is open to the public on weekends only—12 noon to 4 p.m. During the spring a sculpture exhibit is also on display in the garden.

Single season gardens can be an open and shut case, or they can become a garden with a past, present, and future. McCrillis is an excellent example of a single season garden that is beautiful because attention has been given to the needs of the plants of the past and to future growth which lies in the addition of new specimens to enhance and extend the season. Great changes will not be made, but the pleasure of the garden will become extended across the entire growing season.

Prince George's Butterfly Garden

With sweet smells to woo the winged beastie

The best of two worlds meets in the Prince George's Butterfly Garden in the Cosca Regional Park near Clinton. Gardeners or butterfly collectors, and followers of both persuasions, can pursue their interest in this newest small garden. Chris Wagnon, park naturalist and curator of the garden at the Clearwater Nature Center, has established this special-purpose garden.

Flowers are planted solely for the purpose of attracting butterflies, particularly the Baltimore Checkerspot Butterfly, *Euphydryas phaeton*, the Maryland state insect. It also draws those people who follow after winged bits of rainbow.

Some gardens are large for the plants within need the space. This garden is not large; it is a condensed way station with concentrated plantings. As gardening by example, this is surely a blue ribbon winner. The layout of the plots provides two-legged visitors close range for viewing. The robust bloom of the plants dotted with winged diners attests to a successful venture. The beds are interlaced with woodchip-surfaced paths allowing the butterfly watchers a close approach.

Begun in 1985, the new garden was planted primarily with perennials the first year; more annuals appeared the second year. Although it was a new garden, 36 butterfly specimens were spotted in the first summer.

An eighth of an acre is not much ground, but a lot of concentrated attraction is held within.

Only three seasons old in 1987, the garden is not well known yet. However, this will be a must for butterfly enthusiasts and certainly will be interesting for those gardeners who would like to attract these flying flowers to their own garden. All of the plants have been selected to attract butterflies. This is an opportunity to see the plants and the insects in living relationship.

Cameras replace nets when the butterfly collector enters this garden stalking a dab of color as it goes flitting from blossom to blossom. Who might be found visiting today? As is true for the bird watcher, the best game is that which has not yet been spotted. Of course, the prize will be sighting the Baltimore Checkerspot. The Checkerspot is not all that common and never strays far from its favorite food plant, turtlehead, *Chelone glabra*. Unfortunately, it has not been among the butterflies counted so far.

If it is true that waving a red flag attracts a bull, it is also true that planting red flowers will attract butterflies. It is possible to see them alter course by as much as 90 degrees in flight after sighting a garden with red flowers. They are not interested in all red flowers, however. For example, red salvia attract them, but they will not visit. Red zinnias, on the other hand, will attract and support the visitors. Having been attracted to the garden with red flowers, they will visit the other nearby flowers that have nectar or choice sites for egg-laying.

The arrangement of the "butterfly beds" sets shrubs or taller perennials in the center plants of descending height along the outside. This pyramid of bloom in beds no deeper than three to four feet permits close observation. Butterfly Bush, *Buddleia davidii*, and hybrids (shrub) and Butterfly Weed or Butterfly Milkweed, *Asclepias tuberosa* (a perennial), as well as common zinnias are winners with the butterfly crowd. It is easy to see why formal names are needed to keep out the confusion instituted in the application of the same common name to different plants. Yarrow, *Achillea millefolium*, is a plant under debate; some proponents say the butterflies like them and others say they do not.

In addition to flowers for nectar, stiff stalks to winter over on, and the proper greenery for the larva to feed upon, butterflies also need a butterfly bath. This is not a cement-poured item, but rather remnants of a nice mud puddle. Butterflies, being small, could drown in water; they just need a wet spot to sip from.

Some of the plants that the butterflies like also like to have their feet wet; Joe-Pye-weed, Cardinal Flower, and turtlehead need to have a naturally damp ground. The semibog conditions that support these plants provide the attractive—to butterflies—damp places in which to get a drink.

While there are some butterflies all during the growing season, late summer witnesses a full succession of blossoms and a crowd of fluttering wings. For those who also wish to see the eggs, growing caterpillars, and/or chrysalises, all that is required is time, patience, and sharp eyes.

Flowers For a Butterfly Garden

Good Providers of Nectar

Aster
Bee balm
Black-eyed susans
Boneset
Buddelia (butterfly bush)
Chaste tree
Common Milkweed
Coreopsis
Daisy
Dandelion
Daylily
Dogbane
Globe amaranth
Goldenrod
Hyssop
Joe-pye-weed
Lantana
Lilac
Lobelia
Orange milkweed
Phlox
Red geranium
Scabiosa
Sedum sps
Sumac
Sweet alyssum
Tithonia
Verbenas
Wild bergamot
Zinnia

Food Sources

Alfalfa
Beans
Carrot
Cassia
Celery
Cresses
Dill
Dock
Hawthorn
Hibiscus
Hollyhock
Lupine
Mallow
Nasturtium
Nettles
Parsley
Paw paw
Pearly everlastings
Plantain
Sorrel
Spice bush
Wild senna

Good Providers of Both Nectar and Food

Clover
Buckwheat
Milkweed
Thistle

NOTES AND DIRECTIONS

Brighton Dam Gardens

Hours: Daylight

Season: Mid April - end of May

Services: A golf cart is available for the elderly and the handicapped. The road is not paved and is not accessible for the wheelchair-bound visitor. Automobiles are allowed containing elderly or handicapped visitors during weekdays only.

Admission: None

Information: Picnic areas are closed during blooming season because of the need for parking for garden visitors. Peak blooming season information is available by telephone. Gardens are closed the rest of the year. For escort by golf cart for the elderly and handicapped, please call.

Phone: (301) 774-9124

Directions:

From Baltimore:

From the Baltimore Beltway, take Exit 27 or Exit 28 west to Route 29. Turn south on Route 29 to Route 108. At Route 108, turn right (west to Clarksville). In Clarksville turn right on Ten Oaks Road and follow for 0.6 miles where it is joined by Brighton Dam Road on the left. Turn left on Brighton Dam Road and proceed 3.3 miles until you come to the Brighton Dam Parking area on the left.

From Columbia:

Take route 108 west to Clarksville. Proceed from Clarksville as directed from Baltimore.

From Washington:

From the Washington Beltway take Exit 25, New Hampshire Avenue (Maryland Route 650) north. Follow Route 650 through Colesville, Ashton, and Brinklow to Brighton Dam Road. Turn right on Brighton Dam Road and continue 1.1 miles to the Brighton Dam parking area on the right.

Christ Church Biblical Garden

Hours: Daylight

Season: Spring is the best time

Admission: None

Information: Open facilities - no stairs - no refreshments available

Phone:

Directions:

From Washington:

From the Washington Beltway, take Exit 11 south to Route 4. Continue south on Route 4 to Prince Frederick and continue 3 miles past Prince Frederick to the sign on the right to Broome Island Road. Turn right, go about 0.5 mile. Church and garden are on the left side of the road.

From Baltimore:

Take route 2 via Annapolis to Sunderland, MD. At Sunderland, Routes 2 and 4 become one. Continue on Route 4 to sign on right to Broome Island Road. Turn right, go about 100 yards. Church and garden are on the left side of the road.

Ladew Topiary Gardens

Hours: T - F, 10 a.m. - 4 p.m.; Sat., Sun., 12 noon - 5 p.m. Closed Mondays

Season: Mid April - October 31

Services: Group tours open by appointment; arrangements must be made for the cafe.

Admission: Fee

Information: It is especially important to make arrangements in advance if a visit to the house, lunch, and/or an evening concert are anticipated. Days and hours for the house and garden are the same. Visitors should call for day/time for concerts.

This garden is one that visitors would do well to call ahead of time, especially if they are going in a group or traveling a considerable distance. In addition to entering and walking about the garden, they may use the luncheon room (if it is not already engaged), visit the house, and/or listen to a concert. Groups of handicapped visitors might also want their organizer to be particularly careful to call and discuss the limitations of the individuals and/or the garden.

Phone: (301) 557-9466 general information, (301) 557-9570 for groups and other information

Directions:
From Baltimore:

From the Baltimore Beltway, take Exit 27 north on Route 146. Passing Route 145 in Jacksonville continue for 5 miles on Route 146. Ladew Topiary Gardens are on the right.

(These driving directions should not be confused with the mailing address which is 3535 Jarrettsville Pike, Monkton, MD 21111.)

Lilypons Water Gardens

Hours: M - Sat., until 5 p.m.; Sun. 12 Noon until 5 p.m.

Season: Closed: Easter, Christmas Eve through January 1. Not open weekends October through February. July through August is the best garden time.

Admission: None

Information: No easy access to facilities except during the Koi Festival and Lotus Blossom Festival. Three holidays: Lilypons Day, Koi Festival, Lotus Blossom Festival

Phone: (301) 874-5133

Directions:
From Frederick:

Take Route 85 south, approximately 8 miles, to Lilypons Road. There is a white sign on the right side of the road directing to Lilypons Road on the left. Turn left on Lilypons Road, travel 1 mile, turn into drive on the left. The building is set well back and approached via a winding drive.

From Baltimore:

From the Baltimore Beltway (I-695) take Route 70 west to Frederick. Exit at the Route 85 south and proceed as from Frederick.

From Washington:

From the Washington Beltway (I-495) take Route 270 north to Urbana (south of Frederick). Take Route 80 west for 1.5 mi. to Park Mills Road. Turn left on Park Mills Road to Lilypons Road (3.5 miles). Turn right on Lilypons Road for 0.5 mile and turn right into the drive.

McCrillis Gardens

Hours: Garden is open from 10 a.m. till sunset

Season: April, May, and June

Services: Weddings may be arranged

Admission: None

Information: Parking is a problem if you wish to come other than weekends or after 4 p.m.. No parking in the grounds. Parking allowed only at the Woods Academy weekends and after 4 p.m. Not the best for the wheel-chair-bound. No facilities when the Gallery is not open

Phone: (301) 949-8231

Directions:

From Washington:

From the Washington Beltway take exit 36 south toward Washington. At Greentree Road turn right. At the "Y" with Fernwood Road, bear to the left. Watch for the Woods Academy on the right. McCrillis is directly across on the left. Parking is available at the school on weekends and after 4 p.m..

Prince George's Butterfly Garden

Hours: Daylight

Season: May through September

Admission: None

Information: Facilities at the Nature Center closed on Mondays; April - October the Nature Center is open 8:30 a.m. - 4 p.m., Tuesday - Sunday. It is closed Sundays in winter. Wood chip paths not recommended for the wheelchair-bound.

Phone: (301) 297-4575

Directions:

From Baltimore:

Take the Baltimore-Washington Parkway to the Washington Beltway south toward Andrews Air Force Base to Exit 7A (Route 5 South) to Route 223. Turn right on Route 223 to Clinton. Travel 1 mile on Route 223 and turn left onto Brandywine Road (Route 381). Take Thrift Road to the right which enters immediately into the Regional Park.

From Washington:

Clearwater Nature Center is in the Cosca Regional Park in southern Prince George's County, 7.6 miles from the Beltway. Take Exit 7A (Route 5 south) to Route 223. Turn right on Route 223 to Clinton. At Brandywine Road (Route 381), turn left. Take Thrift Road to the right which enters immediately into the Regional Park.

Within the park you will pass power lines, entry to a police station, and playground area. You will then cross a creek. The entrance to the Nature Center will be on your right. The Butterfly Garden is on the right just before the entrance to the Nature Center.

CHAPTER SEVEN
Two For a Day

Several of the gardens within this small book could be combined for day trips. Appendix A has a key to those gardens that would make good day trips. There are six gardens in this chapter that would make up three such trips: Miller House Garden and the Mable Walter Arboretum, both in Hagerstown; Brookside and the Garden of the Washington Temple outside the Washington Beltway; and Sinking Springs and Mount Harmon in Cecil County.

HAGERSTOWN

Hagerstown marks the northwestern limit of the public gardens in Maryland. There were no gardens located farther west. In spite of the dearth of gardens beyond Hagerstown, it is fortunate that it has both an arboretum and a classic townhouse garden of the 19th century. The arboretum is at the Hagerstown Junior College and is spread all over the campus. The townhouse garden is the only garden described in this book where it is mandatory to go through the house. However, the garden is so very representative of its type that it was included. This community displays a generosity of heart and interest in its heritage and its gardens.

The Mable R. Walter Arboretum

Guided by a resolute hand
a garden—for the people—by the people

It is nice to be given a large area of land with the task of preserving the natural beau-

ty and increasing the overall attraction. When the Hagerstown Junior College moved to its new 187-acre campus in 1966, that was the task set before the Campus Beautification Committee. Dr. Mable Walter, chairman of the committee and one of the founders of the junior college, had arrived in the academic world by dint of hard work, entering the teaching arena by means of a one-room school house. By 1970, Dr. Walter's committee instituted the arboretum as the project that would fulfill the goals of beautification and education.

In the beginning, not everyone involved agreed that an arboretum was necessary, but Dr. Walter was very persuasive. Her persuasiveness was all to the good as time passed because funds were extremely short for such an ambitious goal. The very lack of funds for the arboretum worked to the good of communal unity. By enlisting individuals and groups, Dr. Walter helped the arboretum to become interwoven into the fabric of the community. Where individuals could help, she enlisted them. Where more hands were needed she recruited groups. Small projects and individual gardens were put in the hands of groups such as the garden clubs. Every tree, shrub, and garden on campus is there because someone or some group within the community decided to purchase the plant material and see to its inclusion in the grounds.

Funds for public uses need not be structured or out of public coffers to be administered well. Neither is the availability of public funds the only way to create a community project. Private individuals, their own funds, their resources, and their two hands dedicated to the public good can carve out lovely things for the common good, as they did in the arboretum at the Hagerstown Junior College.

This arboretum is certainly the most striking example of the effort of one purposeful woman to march forward with determination, persuasion, and not much else. In the process, she gained a great deal for the people around her, who had not even been aware of what they were missing. Accolades for Dr. Mable Walter came from the community as well as from members of the junior college.

This garden of surprises is worth no less than a half-day. The visit should not be hurried. From the deep thrums of a grandfather frog in the Marsh Garden to the miniature white violets in the Rock Garden, from the velvety curve of a glorious rose to the twisted ruffles of a Japanese arborvitae, the sights and sounds of the Mable R. Walter Arboretum are a quiet experience. The result of combined funds, labor, and love is a crazy-

quilt of gardens and specimen trees across the campus. Thirty-five gardens, large and small, spread over the available 187-acre grounds present a lovely place to walk, study, and visit. Gardens are tucked in the most unexpected places, in folds of buildings, set upon a rocky outcrop, nestled in a natural sink, or spread like a blanket upon the side of a hill. They provide study and research for the student, sanctuary for the wildlife, and pleasure for the visitor.

Depending upon the season, viewing by car may or may not be feasible. In the early spring when apple and other trees are in bloom, a mobile tour would be enjoyable. For the most part, a casual foot-tour is best. Wide-paved paths and roads make many of the gardens of the arboretum available to all. However, some of the gardens are set back into the lawn and are less accessible.

Points of special interest in the arboretum include:

• Founders Hill
• Japanese Tea Garden
• Marsh Garden
• Thieblot Garden
• Rose Garden.

Among the tree specimens in the arboretum, the most worthy of the viewer's attention is not the most beautiful. The Osage Orange or Hedge Apple, *Maclura pomifera* remains in a partial row from its earlier position in a hedgerow. It is a reminder of the past when the farmers divided their fields with living fences and used the orange and golden wood for stout fences of man's making. While the entire arboretum is well worth seeing, the two areas that should not be missed are the Marsh Garden and the Japanese Tea Garden.

BUTTERFLY WEED: Sotterley Plantation Garden ▲
Standing in the summer sun, signalling to butterflies passing by, Orange milkweed presents its colorful clothespin blossoms for pollination. The unusual arrangement of the petals causes the pollinating insect to work at its chore of pollen and nectar collection. If the bee or butterfly is not careful and/or quick, it may find a wing, limb, or antenna caught by the released petals.

GREAT SPANGLED FRITILLARY: Prince George's Butterfly Garden ▶
The butterfly poses for its photograph without a trace of self-consciousness. The butterflies at the Prince George's Butterfly Garden seem not the least alarmed at two-legged visitors armed with cameras.

RED ATTRACTS ▶▶
A female Eastern Tiger Swallowtail is attracted to the nourishment to be found in a vibrant red zinnia growing in the Prince George's Butterfly Garden.

WAXEN POINTS: LILIPONS WATER GARDENS ▲
The early morning light shines back from the leathery surfaces of the leaves and the fuchsia petals of a water lily at Lilypons Water Gardens. The lily ponds are home to the water lilies, koi (Japanese carp), and other waterside inhabitants. The presence of beautiful birds adds to the beauty of the garden.

LOVE-IN-A-MIST: CHRIST CHURCH BIBLICAL GARDEN ◄
Nigella damascena, a resident of the Christ Church Biblical Garden, presents a pretty white blossom surrounded by a feathery froth of green. Native to the Mediterranean, it grows happily and reseeds readily.

KOROMO SHIKIBU: MCCRILLIS AZALEA GARDEN ►
This beautiful lavander azalea has an interesting shape and spider form. It is listed as a Krume and is one of the many different types of azaleas in the McCrillis Azalea Garden.

WINDOWS AND WALLS: LADEW TOPIARY GARDENS ▲

A wall of topiary with windows and a doorway presents a background for the Iris Garden. The iris in the garden are divided by a small stream and companioned with day lilies.

EMPTY CHAIR: McCRILLIS AZALEA GARDEN ◄◄

An invitation to sit in the colorful peace of McCrillis Azalea Garden is given by this empty chair. The gardens are accented by art work during the summer. Beautiful settings to call the visitor forward through the garden are on all fronts.

WOODLAND CARPET: BRIGHTON DAM AZALEA GARDEN ◄

For a very brief period the azaleas at Brighton Dam are breathtaking. Varied types yield a gradual display in this single-season garden. At the peak of bloom, they provide a veritable carpet of color beneath the canopy of trees.

GROWING ARRANGEMENT: BROOKSIDE GARDENS ▲
These members of the primrose family are part of a striking display combined with driftwood and stone. The purple flowers play peek-a-boo beneath the foliage of a companion.

GLISTEN: WASHINGTON TEMPLE ARBORETUM ◀
Reflections of light bounce off the gleaming surface of dogwood berries in the fall. Their stay on the trees at the Washington Temple is brief for the berries are a favorite food for birds and squirrels.

WHITE TOWERS: BROOKSIDE GARDENS ▶
Columns of white chrysanthemums, dazzling in the fall light, are just one of the many forms of the chrysanthemums at the conservatory. A year and a quarter go into the development of chrysanthemums for the Thanksgiving display.

BORAGE, *Borago officinalis:* Sinking Springs Herb Garden ▲
Blue star flowers at Sinking Springs are beautiful enough to eat. At one time they were made into a conserve for the consumptive. History reports borage to be the source of happiness.

CUCUMBER PUMP: Miller House Garden ◄
Plump, white, and handy, this cucumber pump at the Miller House is an antique in the garden world.

ROCK GARDEN: Mable Walter Arboretum ▶
Working with what you have is one way of enhancing your surroundings. Natural stone outcroppings at the Mable Walter Arboretum are perfect for providing the exact surroundings needed for rock garden inhabitants.

PINK AND GREEN: Mount Harmon Plantation
A small circular lily pond sits amid the green boxwood garden of Mount Harmon Plantation. Rosy pink brick walks and walls divide and enclose the garden.

The Marsh Garden

The entire campus is an outdoor class-room, but the Marsh Garden best exemplifies the growth, development, and study that continue in the arboretum. Starting with a deep cleft in the area but without a natural pond, a dam was created with the beginnings of a pond fed by means of a well. Once the pond was established, the shore line could be planted and pond life could be studied. Reeds, grasses, and cattails, all loving to have their feet wet, were soon right at home sheltering the frogs and other small animals who lived there. The frogs and small animals, in turn, caught the attention of the waterside birds who find them necessary for their diet. Each member of plant life and wildlife filled its niche to full capacity. The edges of the pond developed into a full-fledged marsh, and classroom study and research marched apace with it.

Currently the pond is aging and, without assistance, would silt in completely, losing its ability to sustain the marsh plants and the animals that live there. It would become a meadow. Left unchecked, the meadow would acquire trees and woodland would follow. The pond, being a good classroom idea in the beginning, is no less a good classroom now. Steps are being taken to dredge the pond of some of the silt that has infiltrated it, thus slowing down the aging process. Standing at the side of the marsh, listening to the booming of one of the old bullfrogs and watching the gentle sway of cattails in the breeze, one hopes the college is successful in its efforts to keep the pond/marsh garden in its prime.

Japanese Tea Garden

Within a rectangular courtyard of the Ca-reers Building at the junior college is a small garden packed with material for contemplation. Certainly it poses a philosophy different from that of the North American farmland in which it is located. The Japanese Tea Garden was presented to the arboretum by the Foundation of the Hagerstown Chapter of Zonta International. This is one example of how the arboretum has become the community site for dedicating memorials. Permanent plaques in bronze cite dates and dedications.

Complete with an authentic cedar teahouse, this dry landscape representative of mountains and valleys exudes peace and harmony. Dogwood trees and miniature scarlet maples add a splash of color among the green of pine and bamboo. Each bonsai planting is a study in contemplation. The time and devotion that went into the creation of each of these living bonsai stories are to be admired. The lesson they teach the observer is one of patience and dedication, an apt lesson at an educational institution.

Victor Davis Miller III Garden

An Early Nineteenth Century Garden

In the heart of Hagerstown stands a typical townhouse of the late Federal period. Originally built by the J. Bell family in 1818, the house was later owned and named after a local physician, Dr. Miller. William Price, an early owner, added to the early house, establishing the mansion where his first son was born and finally transferring the property to Dr. Miller in 1912. The house was occupied by the Miller family for more than half a century. It remained in the Miller family until after the death of Mrs. Miller when it was acquired by the Washington County Historical Society. A committee representing the Historical Society and the Washington

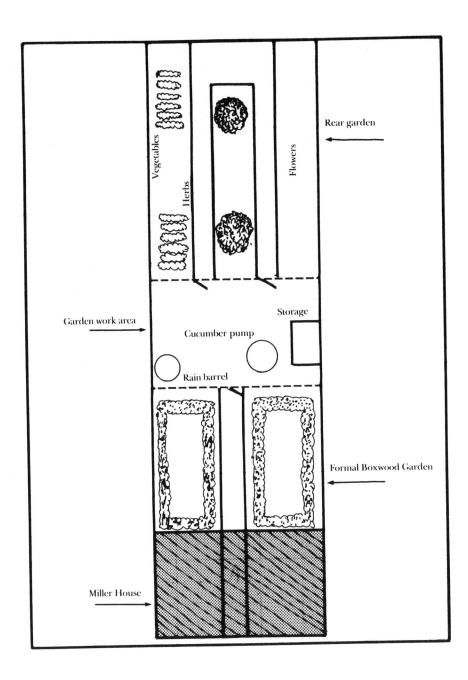

Vegetables

Herbs

Flowers

Rear garden

Garden work area

Cucumber pump

Storage

Rain barrel

Formal Boxwood Garden

Miller House

VICTOR DAVIS MILLER III GARDEN

County Council of Garden Clubs undertook restoration of the garden.

Directly behind the house and sandwiched in between the house and the stable (rebuilt), a dwarf garden of handkerchief proportions cannot be divorced from the accompanying house. The size of the entire lot is but 40 feet by 240 feet. The house occupies the front, the garden the middle, and the stable the rear. The diminutive proportions of the garden in no way lessen its beauty or interest. As one might examine the delicate detail of an antique miniature, it is thus possible to view this 19th-century town garden.

Approached through the Miller House, the garden is first viewed from the rear porch. Typical of small rear gardens of town homes, it is long and narrow. From front to back, the small yard is divided into three sections with the first and the third sections considerably larger than the second section. The center and smaller third contain the work area. It is surprising to find a yard which is too small to allow a motorized lawn mower, to be further divided and have separating fences and shrubs bordering the beds.

A brick wall marches along the sides of the yard setting apart the enclosure in a very private way. At the same time, the walls provide support for the espaliered trees and vines. A brick walkway and white picket fencing separate the gardens.

The first section nearest the house is the formal garden, comprised of two beds bordered with boxwood. Within the beds, bulbs are succeeded by bedding plants. The rear garden has herb and vegetable beds, espaliered fruit trees, and grape vines.

Between the formal garden and the rear garden is a work area complete with a cucumber pump and a water barrel. The cucumber pump is about five feet tall with mechanical parts for the water pump encased in a white painted wooden housing. The housing is shaped with a tapered top giving the whole the resemblance of an overgrown white cucumber with the pumping handle sticking out of one side and the wooden spigot out of another. For those who have never seen a cucumber pump or encountered a water barrel outside of the movie screen, it is interesting to note that they can still be used. In restoring the garden, the brick for one wall and pavement came from donations as did the limestone stepping stones and the plump, white pump.

Not a garden for crowds, the Miller Garden is rather a retreat, an oasis in town. While not a large enough garden to drive a considerable distance to see by itself, the garden is not to be missed if the opportunity presents itself. A trip to see the Miller Garden and the Mable R. Walter Arboretum would make a completely satisfying day.

WASHINGTON BELTWAY–NORTH

Residents of the Washington metropolitan area have an abundance of places to go and things to do, whatever their interest. Men and women who are gardeners themselves or who simply like to look at gardens have a very nice collection of gardens from which to choose. There are two gardens outside the northern side of the Washington Beltway that are breathtaking in their loveliness. Brookside Gardens in Wheaton Regional Park and the gardens of the Washington Temple, combine formal and informal atmospheres.

One of the most common and popular activities to take place in these public gardens are weddings. Brookside has a long list of brides waiting for their turn to get married in the garden. A long wait and the need to plan for a back-up site in case of bad weather do not deter the brides. Lucky is the bride that the sun finds in the garden.

Thousands of people streaming past the Washington Temple Gardens glance upward at the spires glistening in the sunlight, and never think of the peace, quiet, and beauty they are missing. Hidden by the trees at the base of the temple is an arboretum of outstanding beauty. Within is a reflecting pool gleaming like a diamond, a spill of azaleas down a wooded slope, quiet walks, and October Glory red maples.

It is desirable to combine these two gardens in one day-trip. They are only a short distance apart and present a nice contrast of formal and informal gardens. For such a day, lunch in the Wheaton Regional Park might be called for. Also, ladies visiting the Washington Temple Gardens may want to wear skirts instead of slacks since most visitors there are fairly well dressed.

Brookside Gardens

Gardens for the on and off season visitor

Brookside Gardens in the Wheaton Regional Park in Montgomery County is under the Maryland National Capital Park and Planning Commission, a bicounty agency. North of the Washington Beltway, Brookside is within an hour's reach of almost anywhere in the Washington area.

The fifty-acre gardens, open since 1969, are titled a public display garden, but they combine the attributes of an arboretum and a conservatory as well. The use of the gardens across the year is expanded by the presence of a conservatory, a library, and meeting rooms on the grounds. Classes and programs are designed to make the fullest use of the lovely series of gardens.

A unique flavor of Japanese art seems attached to the gardens and this is intentional, if not authentic, even though the landscape architect was German. The oriental air is derived mostly from the presence of a Japanese Tea House and the annual display of Japanese cascade chrysanthemums during November when the conservatory is filled with those flowers in varied forms.

Most gardens are beautiful during the growing season and are easy to love when they are in full bloom and the grass is green. It takes a special something to arouse interest when the snow lies on the ground and mists rise off the stream. Brookside Gardens are lovely to look at spring, summer, fall, and winter.

Maryland weather during the fall and winter is characteristically unlovely: rain, mist, and grey skies, cold and windy. When a rare day comes along with the sky open and blue, the temperature balmy, and the very air sparkling with an invitation to the out-of-doors, the question becomes, where to go? Brookside is an easy answer for the metropolitan resident.

Some Special Gardens at Brookside

A display rose garden features accredited All-American Rose Selections marked with green All-American-Selection labels. Approximately forty varieties are displayed among over 600 plants. Here the visitor can view a candidate for his or her own garden. How large a specimen is it? What is the flower's appearance and fragrance like? Those who just like to come and look have an abundance of material to feast their eyes on and to photograph. During the blooming season, the rose garden is studded with photographers as well as butterflies.

The fragrance garden is truly a garden of

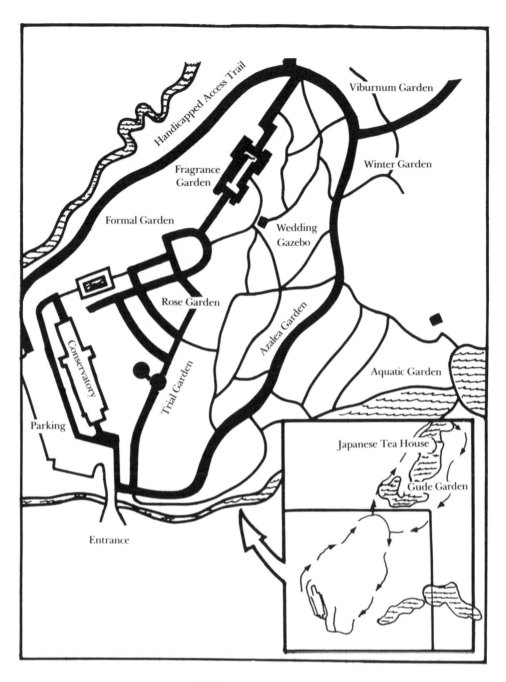

BROOKSIDE GARDENS

the senses. While Brookside's educational programs are well worth attending, the children's program on herbs is especially so. Here visitors of all ages can taste mints while seeing before them the plants that lend themselves to mint flavoring in candies and gum. They can look at the lavender blossoms and learn that lavender is used in soaps and perfume as well as sachets. The lamb's ears plant with its soft green color and white woolly hairs holds the dew in sparkling pearls inviting the visitor to gently stroke the soft surface with a fingertip. Herbs go a long way back in the history of man. They were used for medicine, refreshing drinks, and dyes. Dyes do not necessarily come from exotic plants. Onions can be used to dye Easter eggs or fabric. Some textile fibers respond differently to the dye than do others. With wool, the onion skins dye burnt orange, but yellows, brown, and brass colors can also be obtained from onion skins when combined with other fibers. Flowers of hollyhocks produce pastel shades. Pot Marigold, *Calendula officinalis*, the poor man's saffron, was brought over with the colonists. It can be used fresh or dried to color custards, cream sauces, or puddings.

Also in Brookside, the Gude Garden was awarded top honors in 1977 by the American Association of Nurserymen. This is a garden of gently rolling hills and flowing ponds. Spring brings a rainbow of color that can be viewed from the Japanese Tea House. Azaleas and their larger rhododendron cousins join other shade-loving trees and shrubs in the azalea garden. Under a canopy of native oaks and pines, they make a beautiful spring display. The main bulb display in the Formal, Trial, and Fragrance Gardens as well as a large collection of daffodils in the Azalea Garden draw thousands of visitors each spring.

At all times of the year, Brookside Gardens are beautiful to walk through. The visitor cannot help but relax and be at peace within these gently flowing greens. They are most appreciated in the fall and winter when seasonal change has reduced the offerings of nature and garden. Spring and fall weddings in the open air gazebo at Brookside are popular, although receptions are not held in the gardens. Even so, brides are not averse to signing up six months in advance (as well as preparing a backup location in case of rain) in order to be married amid the beauty of Brookside Gardens.

With two large and two small bodies of water to stroll beside, Brookside is well-named. Gently flowing water adds a cooling element during the heat of the summer days, and little bridges lead the visitor over the trickling stream to visit waterside blossoms.

During the rare late fall or winter day when the weather is trying to make up for gloom and glower, the gardens overflow with house-bound visitors. The conservatory is the central attraction, although the gardens have a beauty in their winter array.

One fall display recommended for anyone wanting to do something special for the Thanksgiving weekend is a visit to the chrysanthemum display in the Brookside Conservatory. A year and a quarter is spent in preparing for the chrysanthemum display in November. Chrysanthemums are displayed in every shape and style in the conservatory, trained on frames, trailing, cascading, large and small, with colors borrowed from the rainbow.

The gardens in their winter attire and the conservatory wear well when the days grow short. Close proximity allows ready access for the Washington metropolitan residents when short days require a minimum of travel time.

The Washington Temple Gardens

The golden spires of the Washington Temple are beacons to all who travel the northern side of the Washington Beltway. Few people know that they are also beacons to one of the most beautiful gardens in the metropolitan area. Only a few years old, the growth attained by these gardens has been remarkable. Development of the landscaping was begun as the building of the temple was coming to a close in the early 1970s.

Situated around the spectacular Mormon Temple, the Washington Temple Gardens need to be very special to keep the visitor's eyes on the ground rather than on the brilliant structure above. Because it is the setting of an awe-inspiring structure and the church grounds, many potential visitors are unaware of its availability to the public.

In a city with many structures whose gates restrict the inflow of the uninvited, gates at the Washington Temple might be seen by some as a rebuff. They are not marked with a welcome sign, but the guard at the gatehouse is very friendly and happy to give directions to parking and the gardens. The purpose of these gardens is threefold: to beautify the temple; to provide a lovely, peaceful area for meditation; and to hide a very large parking lot. They fulfill these tasks admirably.

Parking to see the gardens is, in itself, an exercise in garden exploration. Disguised by a garden of trees, shrubs, and beds, a very large parking lot sits in immediate proximity to the entry of the temple without calling attention to its presence or size. Within this parking lot is the mall, a long walkway running from the base of the parking area to the entry for the temple. October Glory red maples are planted to the sides among the parking isles. This is the area's largest October Glory maple collection. Shrubs, planting beds, and a circular pool which displays a dancing spike of water in its center, lie along the walks. This is but one of the lovely spots to be enjoyed even if only in passing, and certainly a place to see with its fall color.

Although situated very close to the Washington Beltway, the trees beyond the perimeter of the gardens effectively screen the viewer from the sights of traffic and almost eliminate the sounds generated by its flow. The diversity of plantings provides interesting viewing all year and the grounds are open year round. The gardens range from more formal plantings, such as those around the reflecting pool, to the informal as displayed in the azalea beds that wander down the slope toward the Beltway behind the Temple.

Surely the most photogenic and most photographed site in the gardens is the reflecting pool. Outside the visitors' center and placed just right to catch the beautiful spires on the top of the temple, the reflecting pool is surrounded by a succession of spring bulbs, summer flowers, and chrysanthemums in the fall. A stepping-stone walk allows camera buffs and other visitors the opportunity to catch the view.

Nestled in the angular spaces of the several sides of the temple are cameo gardens with intensive plantings. Beautiful and unusual trees, shrubs, and plants call for the visitor's attention; however, the trees and other plants in these gardens have not always stayed put. Aside from the beauty of the plantings, this is a good garden to see the effect of differing exposures on plants. The mass of the building alters exposure, wind currents, and hours of daylight. A talk with the head gardener, Mr. Ellis Levine, revealed the changes he has made as individual plants (including trees) had to be moved or

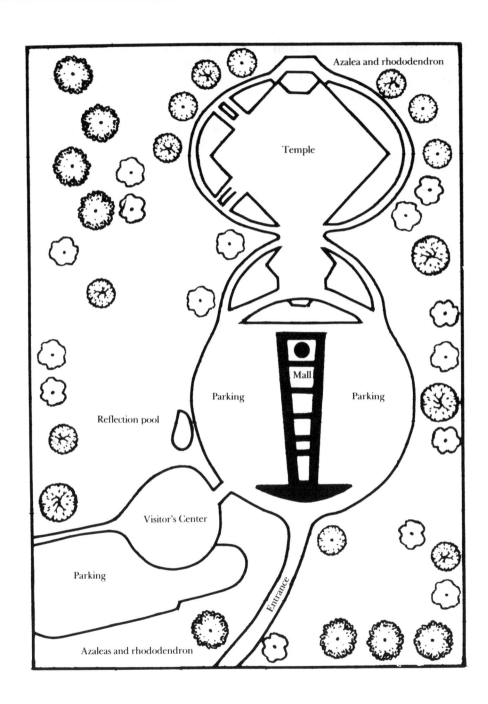

Azalea and rhododendron

Temple

Mall

Parking

Parking

Reflection pool

Visitor's Center

Parking

Entrance

Azaleas and rhododendron

WASHINGTON TEMPLE GARDENS

replaced because of their reluctance to thrive in the location first chosen.

With 25 acres under cultivation and with the impact of the dimensions of the building on the individual garden environment and the plants within, the garden is growing and expects to continue to grow. New plantings are being developed to allow each garden the opportunity to grow successfully and show its best potential.

Several thousand azaleas and rhododendron spilling down the slope in a natural woodland setting in the Temple Gardens proclaim the release from winter and the joy of spring. Fall, however, will not be outdone;

there are darker colors to be sure, but no less brilliant. The beauty of the sourwood with its blazing red color competes with the dogwood bejeweled with glistening red berries. Both have to work hard to compete with the fall beauty of the maples.

On the temple grounds, walks, drives, ramps, and very few steps make this one of the best gardens for the wheelchair-bound visitor. A broad walk surrounding the base of the temple progresses from one garden setting to the next. A visitor center also contains information and restroom facilities. It is a lovely garden to visit, relax in, and gain a measure of peace on earth.

CECIL COUNTY

For a day-trip away from metropolitan areas, take a garden excursion to Cecil County. The countryside is peaceful and the gardens to be seen are tucked away and must be ferreted out. Two gardens of modest size and considerable interest may be visited, Sinking Springs Herb Garden and Mount Harmon Plantation Garden. Pell Memorial Garden, a third and very small garden is about half way between them. Because luncheon is available at Sinking Springs Herb Garden, it makes a nice first stop. Reservations must be made for luncheons that are very refreshing after an instructive morning in the garden. After lunch, a continuation of the trip to Mount Harmon will pass Chesapeake City with the Chesapeake and Delaware Canal Museum and the tiniest of gardens yet, the Pell Memorial Garden. Flowers surround a small gazebo which sits nearly under the bridge and looks out over the canal. Chesapeake City is one of the smallest of Maryland's Cities with one of the smallest of populations and its garden is in keeping with the setting. The boxwood garden at Mount Harmon will

make a peaceful stop before the return trip home. Mount Harmon is reached by traversing a very long, very narrow road reflective of the times when the fastest transportation was by water.

Mount Harmon Plantation

A boxwood garden

In the past, water power for transportation was much faster and smoother than roads, and many plantations were located on water frontage for that reason. Mount Harmon is situated just off the Sassafras River. It should be no surprise to the visitor that the entryway by road is long, tree-shaded, narrow, and not built for speedy traffic. Narrow means that if one car meets another, one of them will have to back up to the nearest wide spot and pull over so the other may pass.

The plantation was created from a landgrant to Godfrey Harmon around 1650. The garden resides next to the manor house that dates from 1730. The property remained in different branches of the family

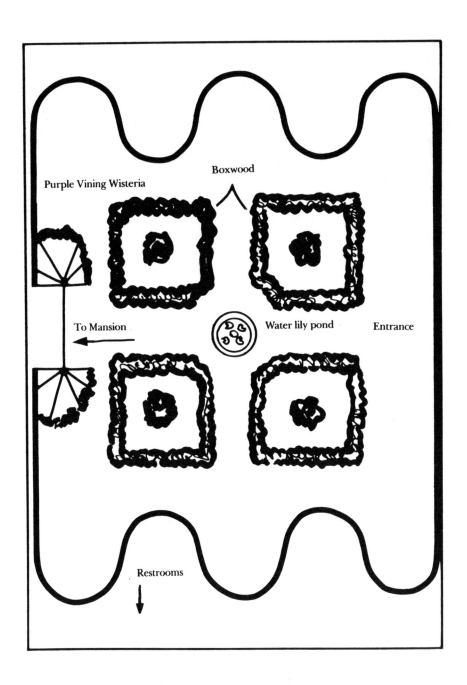

MOUNT HARMON

until 1927 when it was sold to an outsider upon the death of the owner, Sydney G. Fisher. The acreage of the once prosperous tobacco plantation diminished and fields reverted to woodlands in a process ecologists call old field succession. In 1963, Mrs. Harry Clark Boden IV, a direct descendent of families who had lived on the plantation, acquired the property and spent the next twelve years restoring the manor house and its grounds to their former glory. Wanting to be sure of its preservation, she donated the property and a considerable endowment to the National Trust for Historic Preservation.

The garden has been restored to the formality of the 18th century. Nearly square in shape, the garden is approximately a quarter of an acre. It is bicolored pink and green for most of the year, with the green of the boxwood countered by the soft pink brick of the walls and walks.

The walls are straight in line along the back and front of the garden and are combined with serpentine sections along the sides. Looking out over the lower front wall the visitor has a view of the Back Creek. The walled enclosure is trim yet open to view with access from the front via a few steps to the walk and from the rear via a descending pair of curved brick stairs. At the top of the stairs, two English yew trees (*Taxus baccata*, variety *dovastonii*) stand guard between the garden and the drive along the back of the manor house. For more than 200 years, this pair of yew trees has stood sentinel beside the steps to the boxwood garden at the Mount Harmon Plantation. In the center of the garden a small round pool sports a fountain with an alert stone squirrel perched on one side. The walks surround the pool and radiate out to separate the four sections of the garden.

Lavender blossoms of the wisteria create tricolor beauty in the spring. Four tree-form wisteria are the center for each of the four sections of the garden, each enclosed by boxwood. Climbing wisteria grace the wrought iron railing and curve around the central set of stairs at the back wall. The garden would be unrelieved green without the mellow brick wall that, when combined with the walkways, provides a soft warm color as well as line and flow to the eye.

Even if the visitor is not particularly fond of boxwood, this is a striking garden. Its patterns and warm colors along with its peaceful enclosure make it a very restful place.

Sinking Springs

a "Mux'y" herb garden
[mux from Shakespeare's English means a mess]

Deep in the farmland of Cecil County in a most unexpected spot is a charming herb garden. This place is the choice for retirement of a former teacher who is not so far away from his profession. Bill Stubbs is still teaching; instead of teaching history, he now teaches herbs. On land that has been in his family for many years, his herb garden attracts bees, butterflies, and people. With his wife, Ann, who teaches the culinary use of herbs, they spread the word on these most useful plants. The Stubbs have even lectured officials of the Campbell Soup Company in the use of herbs. In the 1970s, they opened their garden to the public.

Sinking Springs' visitors have the pleasure of seeing the herbs in their lush state and hearing of their history and current use. They may enter into the dining room, redolent with the scent of dried herbs and flowers, and sit to enjoy a luncheon perfectly flavored with fresh and dried herbs.

Stone paths mark the pattern of each of the sixteen gardens. The gardens are a mixture of planning and planting by the west wind. Where the west wind has planted favorably, the green guest is allowed to stay and grace the garden with its presence. When the uninvited plants are too numerous, they receive a helping hand to move along. Small statues, a pool, and a fountain add a note of whimsy to these most useful of all plants.

An early morning visit to the garden blends human and bee visitors. Butterflies, ducks, and hummingbird attendees come later. The red flowers of the monarda, a member of the mint family, seem to hum as bees work steadily from blossom to blossom. They are so intent at their task that the visitor may join their ranks with little disturbance. Blue stars stand at the tips of the borage plant, *Borago officinalis.* They are pretty in salads and once were made into conserves to comfort the heart and spirit as they were thought to bring happiness. Lavender stems sway with the weight of the bumblebees. English Lavender, so prized for fragrance in soap and sachets, sends its blossom-lined spikes above the plants. As the morning air warms and oils within the plants become more volatile, the gentle brushing of shoe or cloth against the leaves raises scents through the air giving the garden a wonderfully welcome smell.

A working herb garden is different from a formal, trimmed herb garden. Time for polish is relinquished in favor of time to harvest and care for the herbs which have been gathered. Classes are taught in drying herbs and flowers and in the creation of beautiful handicrafts using the dried materials. Tours are conducted through the gardens at a leisurely pace allowing the visitor to taste, sniff, and feel the texture of the plant at hand.

Unfortunately, early American houses and gardens, after which this is patterned, had neither the space nor facilities for the handicapped. The dining room has limited maneuvering room and the restroom is on the second floor. Ground floor facilities are available in the bed and breakfast cottage for the elderly and the handicapped.

For the visitor who would like to be able to stay and see the gardens from morning to night a guest cottage sits on the perimeter of the gardens facing them. Breakfast is provided by the hosts.

A visit to Sinking Springs Herb Gardens is a very personal trip. The hosts, Bill and Ann Stubbs, are warm, generous people who put full measure into their cup of hospitality. Visitors are welcome to browse through the Mux'n Room and are encouraged to touch the herbs.

Sinking Springs Herb Garden
Sample Menu

Fruity Herbal Punch

Cheese Covered Breast of Chicken on Homemade English Muffin

(Choice of Roquefort or Sharp Cheddar)

Seasoned with Thyme

Fresh Garden Salad with Tarragon Vinegar Dressing

Fresh Vegetable of the Day

Flavored with Appropriate Herb

Homemade Lemon-Balm Coffee Cake

Accented with Lemon Butter

Herb Tea

Reservations Required for Luncheon or Dinner

NOTES AND DIRECTIONS

Brookside Gardens

Hours: Grounds 9 a.m. - Sunset, Conservatory 9 a.m. - 5 p.m. daily.
Closed Christmas day

Season: Year round

Services: Shuttle bus provided to and from distant parking in spring.

Admission: None

Information: Tours, classes

Phone: (301) 949-8230

Directions:
From Washington:

Take exit 31A north to Wheaton (Georgia Avenue) north to Randolph Road, turn right on Randolph Road for 0.3 mi. Turn right onto Glenallan Avenue and travel for 0.6 mi. Brookside Gardens is on the right-hand side.

Mable R. Walter Arboretum

Hours: Daylight

Season: Year round

Services: Tours

Admission: None

Information: Facilities open only when the college is. If the visitor wishes a guide it would be advisable to call ahead of time; otherwise it is permitted to visit the grounds at all times. Some of the gardens are more accessible for the wheel-chair bound visitor than others. The Marsh Garden is not an easy access garden. Address comunications to: Director of the Arboretum, Hagerstown Junior College, 751 Robinwood Drive, Hagerstown, Maryland 21740.

Phone: (301) 790-2800 x 212

Directions:

Hagerstown may be approached from Washington and/or Baltimore via Interstate Route 70. Exit at Hagerstown on Route 40, west on 40, turn right on Robinwood Drive. Hagerstown Jr. College is about three miles on the left hand side of the road .

Mount Harmon Plantation Garden

Hours: Daylight

Season: Open year round, wisteria bloom in early summer.

Admission: None for the garden / Fee for the house

Information: There are a few steps to the garden and accessible facilities for the wheel-chair-bound. Note: House days are limited; visitors should call. Visitors making an extended trip or combining visits to more than one garden should call ahead to make sure of the accessibility of all of the areas to be visited.

Phone: (301) 275-2721

Directions:
From Baltimore:

From the Baltimore Beltway, take Interstate 95 east to Exit 109 (Route 279) south to Elkton. At the intersection of Routes 279 and 213, turn left on Route 213 south. At Cecilton, turn right on Route 282. Proceed 2.5 miles to the fork of Route 282 and Grove Neck Road. (282 bears off to the right). Travel on Grove Neck Road for approximately 2 miles. (Note: Mt. Harmon Plantation sign.)

At the entry to Mt. Harmon, there is an historical marker. Just prior to the Mt. Harmon historical marker is the marker for another site. Mt. Harmon drive is on the left.

Sinking Springs Herb Garden

Hours: Daylight

Season: Mid-July through September

Services: Tours, lectures, luncheons, and dinners by arrangement

Admission: Fee

Information: Call ahead for reservations. Lecture tours available for large groups

Phone:(301) 398-5566

Directions:
From Baltimore:

From the Baltimore Beltway, travel east on Interstate 95 to exit 109 (Route 279). Take Route 279 to Elkton, MD. At the intersection of Routes 279 and 213, turn left on Route 213 south. Travel Route 213 for about 3.8 miles, passing Route 40 intersection, to Route 395 (Locust Point Road) and turn right on Route 395. Take Locust Point Road to Blair Shore Road, which branches off when Locust Point Road turns right. Sinking Springs Herb Farm will be on the left, 2 miles.

Victor Davis Miller III Garden

Hours: W - F, 1 p.m. - 4 p.m.; Sat., Sun, 2 p.m. - 5 p.m. Closed 1st and 2nd weeks of December, January, February, and March.

Season: Spring - early summer

Admission: Fee

Information: Steps must be encountered to enter the house and again to descend to the garden. This presents a considerable barrier for the handicapped visitor, nearly insur-

mountable for the wheelchair-bound. If co-ordinating a trip between gardens, calling ahead of time to make sure of the availability of both gardens is very important.

Phone: (301) 797-8782

Directions:
Hagerstown:

From I-70 in Hagerstown, take Route 40 west (Franklin Street). Go through downtown and turn left on Prospect Street. Go one block, turn left on Washington Street. The Miller House is on the right in the middle of the block.

Address: 135 West Washington St.

Washington Temple Gardens

Hours: T - F, 7 a.m. - 8 p.m.; Sat., 7 a.m. - 6 p.m.; Sun., 2 p.m. - 6 p.m.. Closed Mondays and Christmas

Season: Year round

Admission: None

Information: Note: For two weeks in the summer and two weeks in the winter, the grounds are closed for cleanup and rejuvenation. Groups should make an advance call to confirm that the day they wish to visit will find the grounds open. Restroom facilities are in the visitor center.

Phone: (301) 587-0144

Directions:
From Washington:

From the Washington Beltway (I-495), take exit 35 to Connecticut Ave. The first intersection to the right leads to Sligo Creek Parkway. On Sligo Creek Parkway, continue through the first stop sign and along the drive until it meets with Stonybrook Drive. Turn left. After approximately two blocks, the entrance to the Visitor's Center is on the left with the gates to the grounds just beyond.

APPENDIX A
Garden Tables

This appendix is designed to provide the garden enthusiast with an at-a-glance reference to basic information on the public gardens and arboreta of Maryland.

GARDENS AND THEIR SPECIALTIES

Name	Speciality	Best Month(s)
American Indian Garden	Aboriginal	July Till Frost
Arboretum of Londontown	Multi-Storied	May/July/Nov
Brighton Dam Azalea Garden	Azaleas	May/June
Brookside Gardens	Gardens/Arboretum	May/July/Nov
Christ Church Biblical Garden	Bible Garden	April/May
City of Baltimore Conservatory	Tropical/Seasonal Displays	Easter/Christmas
Cylburn Arboretum	Gardens/Arboretum	Spring/Summer
Farthing's Ordinary	Vegetables/Herbs/Dessert	Summer
Freedom of Conscience Memorial	Annuals/Azaleas	All Season
Garden of Remembrance	Azaleas/Dogwood/Boxwood	All Season
Godiah Spray Plantation Garden	Vegetables/Herbs	Summer
Greenway Arboretum	General/Desert Greenhouse	July/Aug
Hampton National Historic Site	English/Parterre/Cutting	Spring/Fall
Helen Avalynne Tawes Garden	State Sec. Repres. Gardens	All Season
Ladew Topiary Gardens	Topiary	All Season
Lilypons Water Gardens	Waterlilies	July/August
Mable R. Walter Arboretum	Gardens/Arboretum	May
Margaret Brent Memorial Garden	General/Gazebo	June till Frost
McCrillis Azalea Garden	Azaleas/Rhododendrons	April-May-June
Miller House Garden	Gardens in Miniature	May/June
Mount Harmon Plantation Garden	Boxwood/Wisteria	May
Mulberry Shoppe Herb Garden	Herbs	May till Frost
Nat. Col. Farm Kitchen Garden	Kitchen/Herb	June till Frost
Old-Fashioned Rose Garden	Historic Roses	Late May/Early June
Pleasure Gardens of William Paca	Parterre	Three Season
Pr. Geo.'s Co. Butterfly Garden	Butterfly Attraction	August
Sherwood Gardens	Tulips	April/May
Sinking Springs Herb Farm	Herbs	June till Frost
Sotterley Plantation Gardens	Vegetables/Herbs/Dessert	June till Frost
Stillridge Herb Garden	Herbs	June till Frost
St. Mary's College Herb	Herbs	July till frost
The Gardens of the Hist. Soc.	General	Spring/Early Summer
Washington Temple Garden	Arboretum	All season

GARDEN INFORMATION BY COUNTY

County	Name	Approx. Acreage	Handicap Access	Fee
Ann Arundel	Arboretum of Londontown Public House	28	2	$
	Helen Avalynne Tawes Garden	6.0	4	0
	Pleasure Gardens of William Paca	2.0	2	$
Baltimore	Hampton National Historic Site	43.0	1	0
Baltimore City	City of Baltimore Conservatory	2	1	0
	Cylburn Arboretum	176	3	0
	Sherwood Gardens	6.0	2	0
Calvert	Christ Church Biblical Garden	0.1	3	0
Carroll	Greenway Arboretum	27.0	2	$
	Old-Fashioned Rose Garden	0.2	2	$
Cecil	Mount Harmon Plantation Garden	0.3	2	0
	Sinking Springs Herb Farm and Garden	5.0	2	$
Frederick	Lilypons Water Gardens	300.0	1	0
Harford	Ladew Topiary Gardens	22.0	2	$
Howard	Stillridge Herb Garden	6.0	2	0
Montgomery	Brighton Dam Azalea Garden	5	3	0
	Brookside Gardens	50	3	0
	Washington Temple Arboretum	0.1	3	0
	McCrillis Azalea Garden	5.5	2	0
Pr. George's	Nat. Col. Farm Kitchen Garden	0.2	2	$
	Pr. Geo.'s Co. Butterfly Garden	0.1	2	0
St. Mary's	American Indian Garden	0.2	1	$
	Farthing's Ordinary	0.5	2	$
	Freedom of Conscience Memorial	0.1	1	0
	Garden of Remembrance	0.8	2	0
	Godiah Spray Plantation Garden	0.5	2	$
	Margaret Brent Memorial Garden	1.0	2	0
	Sotterley Plantation Gardens	2.0	2	$
	St. Mary's College Herb Garden	0.2	3	0
	Mulberry Shoppe Herb Garden	0.1	3	0
Talbot	The Gardens of the Historical Soc.	0.5	2	0
Washington	Mable R. Walter Arboretum	187.0	2	0
	Miller House Garden	0.1	2	$

* Handicapped access   4 = very good   3 = moderately good   2 = some problems
  1 = impediments

ADDITIONAL GARDEN INFORMATION

Name	Other Historic Structure	Comments
American Indian Garden	No	Day-Trip Itinerary*
Arboretum of Londontown Publik House	Yes	Unfailingly Beautiful
Brighton Dam Azalea Garden	No	Single Season
Brookside Gardens	No	Unfailingly Beautiful
Christ Church Biblical Garden	Yes	
City of Baltimore Conservatory	No	Palm House is Historic
Cylburn Arboretum	Yes	
Farthing's Ordinary	Yes	Day-Trip Itinerary
Freedom of Conscience Memorial	No	Day-Trip Itinerary
Garden of Remembrance	No	Day-Trip Itinerary
Godiah Spray Plantation Garden	Yes	Day-Trip Itinerary
Greenway Arboretum	No	Day-Trip Itinerary
Hampton National Historic Site	Yes	
Helen Avalynne Tawes Garden	No	
Ladew Topiary Gardens	Yes	Unfailingly Beautiful
Lilypons Water Gardens	No	Working Garden*
Mable R. Walter Arboretum	No	Day-Trip Itinerary
Margaret Brent Memorial Garden	No	Day-Trip Itinerary
McCrillis Azalea Garden	Yes	Single Season
Miller House Garden	Yes	Day-Trip Itinerary
Mount Harmon Plantation Garden	Yes	Day-Trip Itinerary
Mulberry Shoppe Herb Garden	No	Day-Trip Itinerary
Nat. Col. Farm Kitchen Garden	Yes	
Old-Fashioned Rose Garden	Yes	Day-Trip Itinerary
Pleasure Gardens of William Paca	Yes	Unfailingly Beautiful
Pr. Geo.'s Co. Butterfly Garden	No	
Sherwood Gardens	No	Single Season
Sinking Springs Herb Farm and Garden	No	Working Garden*
Sotterley Plantation Gardens	Yes	Day-Trip Itinerary
Stillridge Herb Garden	No	Working Garden*
St. Mary's College Herb Garden	No	Day-Trip Itinerary
The Gardens of the Historical Soc.	Yes	
Washington Temple Arboretum	No	Unfailingly Beautiful

* *Not Necessarily Beautiful*

List of Volunteers

Hats off to the volunteers!

The gardens have been unstinting in their praise of the community volunteers who dream dreams of gardens, and work to make those dreams come true. Some have been residents of the community, others have been staff members who worked well beyond the call of the working hours. It is my pleasure to add my praise to that of the curators of the gardens.

American Indian—Farthing's Ordinary—Godiah Spray Garden

The St. Mary's City Commission has ask that recognition and thanks be extended to Historic St Mary's City Staff for their work beyond the call of duty and Volunteers Debra Pence-Massie and Harriet Stout for their efforts in behalf of these gardens.

Brighton Dam Azalea Garden

Mr. Raymond W. Bellamy, Sr.,Former Chairman, WSSC
Mr. Paul H. Hancock, Former Watershed Supervisor, WSSC
Mr. Andrew N. Adams, Jr., Ten Oaks Nursery & Gardens, Inc.
Mr. Michael J. Grear, Watershed Manager, WSSC

Brookside Gardens

The curator of Brookside Gardens has ask that recognition and thanks be extended to all of the Brookside Garden's Volunteers for their devoted hours of labor.

Christ Church

Volunteer work and support have been generously provided by Mr. and Mrs. John H. Dean

Freedom of Conscience Triangle Memorial Garden

The St. Mary's City Commission has ask that recognition and thanks be extended to The Mistress Brent Garden Club for their generous work in behalf the Freedom of Conscience Memorial Garden.

Garden of Remembrance

St. Mary's College has ask that recognition and thanks be extended to the St. Mary's College Alumni for their support of the Garden of Remembrance.

Hampton National Historic Site

The curator of Hampton National Historic Site wished to recognize and thank the members of District III of the Federated Garden Clubs of Maryland, Inc. for their support of Hampton National Historic Site.

Helen Avalynne Tawes Garden

The curators of the Helen Avalynne Tawes Garden have ask that recognition and thanks be extended to the Maryland Department of Natural Resources, Maryland Department of General Services, and members of District II of the Federated Garden Clubs of Maryland, Inc. for their support of the garden.

London Town Publik House & Gardens

Mrs. Nancy Seamon
Mrs. Thomas Morton
Mrs. Mildred Court
Mrs. Sylvia Clarke
The Tidewater Garden Club
The Loch Haven Garden Club
The Holly Berry Garden Club
The Four Rivers Garden Club
The London Town Garden Guides
Friends of the London Town Publik House & Gardens

Margaret Brent Garden

The St. Mary's City Commission has ask that recognition and thanks be extended to The Friends of Margaret Brent for their devoted efforts to the Margaret Brent Garden.

McCrillis Azalea Gardens

The curator of McCrillis Azalea Gardens has ask that recognition and thanks be given to Mr. Robert Barry, Satsuki Azalea Project Chairman and The Brookside Gardens Chapter of the Azalea Society of America for their support of the McCrillis Azalea Gardens.

Miller house

Volunteer work and support have been generously supplied by Mrs. Victor Miller III and Mr. Dennis John Warrenfeltz for the Miller house garden.

Mount Harmon Plantation Boxwood Garden

Mrs. Harry Clark Boden, Mount Harmon Plantation and Natural Lands Trust have provided generous support of the Mount Harmon Plantation Boxwood Garden.

Mulberry Shoppe Herb Garden

Ms. Gale Burwell
Ms. Marian Jones
Ms. Suzanne Lawrence
Ms. Barbara Townsend

National Colonial Farm

Mrs. Marie Lipsie
Mrs. Jeanne Engelhardt
Dr. Donald Strasburg–Entomological Advisor

Old-Fashioned Rose Garden

Boy scout Troop 481
Tommy Batten
Dominic Dattilio
Jayne Dattilio
Karen Dattilio
Lu Dawson
Emil Deckart
Tom Ford
Bob Kimmel
Elizabeth Marshall
Margaret Powers
Ann Pritts
Ann Rasinski
Jean Scott
Ralph Sloan
Karen Soisson
Richard Soisson
Peggy Thornburg
Shane White
Ed Williams

Pleasure Gardens of William Paca Garden

The curator of the Pleasure Gardens of William Paca Garden has ask that the Volunteers of Historic Annapolis, Inc. be recognized and thanked for their generous support of the Pleasure Gardens of William Paca Garden.

Prince George's Butterfly Garden

Alva Worthington
Jack Worthington
Frances Vandivier
Larry Vandivier
Lynn Martin
Lee Martin
Lutheran Brotherhood
Junior Naturalists of Clearwater Nature Center
Maryland-National Capital Park and Planning Commission

Sherwood Gardens

Mr. Richard T. Hale, President of the Guilford Association 1987
Sherwood Gardens Committee:
Mr. Gerard S. Wise, Honorary Chairman
Mrs. Samuel Hopkins, Past Chairman
Mr. Hugh P. McCormick, Past President

Mrs. Frank Shriver Jones, Present (1987) Chairman
Mr. Richard L. Steiner, Member
Mrs. LeRoy E. Kirby, Member
Mr. Philip English, Member
Mrs. Paul C. Nicholson, Jr., Member
Dr. John W. Payne, Member
Mrs. Kenneth L. Grief, Member
Mr. Rowland A. Morrow, Member
Mr. D. Jeffrey Rice, Volunteer
Mrs. John T. KIng, III, Volunteer
Mrs. N. Travers Nelson, Volunteer
Mr. Morton Y. Bullock, III, Volunteer
Mr. & Mrs. Harvey R. Clapp, III, Volunteers
Mr. Walter G. Lohr, Jr., Volunteer
Mr. Thomas P. Perkins, III, Volunteer
Dr. P. Pierce Linaweaver

St. Mary's College Herb Garden

St. Mary's College has ask that recognition and thanks be extended to the St. Mary's County
Garden Club for their support of the St. Mary's College Herb Garden.

The Historical Society Garden, of Talbot County

Mrs. Georgia S. Adler
Mrs. John E. Akridge, III
Mrs. Richard T. Allen
Mrs. L. Bradley Baker
Mrs. William H. Baldwin
Mrs. Attison L. Barnes
Mrs. Charles F. Benson
Mrs. Henry Corbin
Mrs. Philip E.L. Dietz, Jr.
Mrs. Robert Downes, III
Mrs. Roy Fleckenstein
Mrs. Claiborne W. Gooch, III
Mrs. William P. Griffin
Mrs. John A. Hawkinson
Mrs. J. Robert Hopkins
Mrs. John E. Jackson
Mrs. John M. Jelich
Mrs. Roger C. Judd
Mrs. Byron H. LaMotte, Jr.
Mrs. Donald T. Lewers
Mrs. David F. Miller
Mrs. Richard H. Norair

Mrs. Adolph Pretzler
Mrs. David Pyles
Mrs. Doris Rend
Mrs. Kenneth C. Sappington
Mrs. Harry R. Scott
Mrs. Paul C. Stokes
Mrs. David A. Stout
Mrs. W. Moorhead Vermilye
Mrs. J. Warner Whalen
Mrs. Richard K. White, Jr.
Mrs. Clarissa T. White
Mrs. Christopher N. Willits
Mrs. R. Lane Wroth

Washington Temple

The curator of the Washington Temple Arboretum wishes recognition be made for the extensive work provided by the late Irvin J. Nelson—Landscape Architect for the Washington Temple Arboretum.

A few of the gardens did not wish to make a list. When the volunteers are so many it is easy to overlook someone, but they add their thanks to their many supporters of the past, present and future.

City of Baltimore Conservatory
Cylburn Arboretum
Ladew Topiary Garden
Mable R. Walter Arboretum

Appendix C
Tips and Checklist

Trips Abroad—Making Them Work

A successful trip is a joy to the visitor and a reward to the host. Curators of gardens would wish there were no unsuccessful trips for visitors; they would rather have one happy visitor than 20 unhappy visitors.

Finding the garden(s) you wish to visit is the first step. The map on the following two pages has been provided to help you find the general location of the garden(s). A current road map should be used for all detailed route planning. Once you have located the garden, you have some other decisions to make. Depending on the number and composition of the individuals taking the trip, planning may be brief or extensive. Questions the coordinator might want to think about concerning the visitors:

• How many people are going?
• What are their ages and interests?
• How much walking will they tolerate without becoming too tired?
• What kind of a garden do they want to see?
• Are there any visitors who need special assistance?
• Are the visitors going to want to eat?
• What kind of transportation will be needed?

Information, planning, and communication are essential for the success of any trip for an individual, family, or group of unrelated visitors. A good formula for preparing successful garden visiting trips is:

Information + Planning + Communication = A Good Trip

INFORMATION should be gathered on visitors, the intended garden, transportation, necessary dress if applicable, and emergency measures.

PLANNING should be done—concerning the season of the garden to be seen, days/hours open, meals if any, coordination of several gardens, and the unexpected—such as a rain date for bad weather.

COMMUNICATION should be encouraged between the coordinator and the visitors about the garden, and between the coordinator and the garden staff about the visitors to arrive. Additional communication is necessary between adults and children when they are going to a garden about what they are going to see.

After the general information about the garden(s) involved has been gathered, it will be applied differently for families or individuals than for a group of unrelated visitors. A family taking the car will need less planning for the trip itself. If children are involved, however, adults need to do more planning and provide advance information so that everyone will enjoy the outing. Groups of individuals of similar abilities, interests, and ages usually make for a more congenial trip. Elderly or handicapped visitors mixed with small active children can be wearing on both sets.

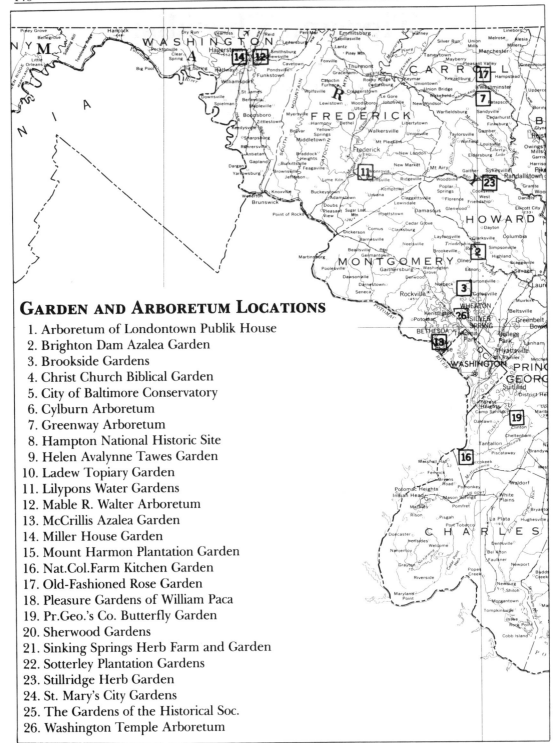

Garden and Arboretum Locations

1. Arboretum of Londontown Publik House
2. Brighton Dam Azalea Garden
3. Brookside Gardens
4. Christ Church Biblical Garden
5. City of Baltimore Conservatory
6. Cylburn Arboretum
7. Greenway Arboretum
8. Hampton National Historic Site
9. Helen Avalynne Tawes Garden
10. Ladew Topiary Garden
11. Lilypons Water Gardens
12. Mable R. Walter Arboretum
13. McCrillis Azalea Garden
14. Miller House Garden
15. Mount Harmon Plantation Garden
16. Nat.Col.Farm Kitchen Garden
17. Old-Fashioned Rose Garden
18. Pleasure Gardens of William Paca
19. Pr.Geo.'s Co. Butterfly Garden
20. Sherwood Gardens
21. Sinking Springs Herb Farm and Garden
22. Sotterley Plantation Gardens
23. Stillridge Herb Garden
24. St. Mary's City Gardens
25. The Gardens of the Historical Soc.
26. Washington Temple Arboretum

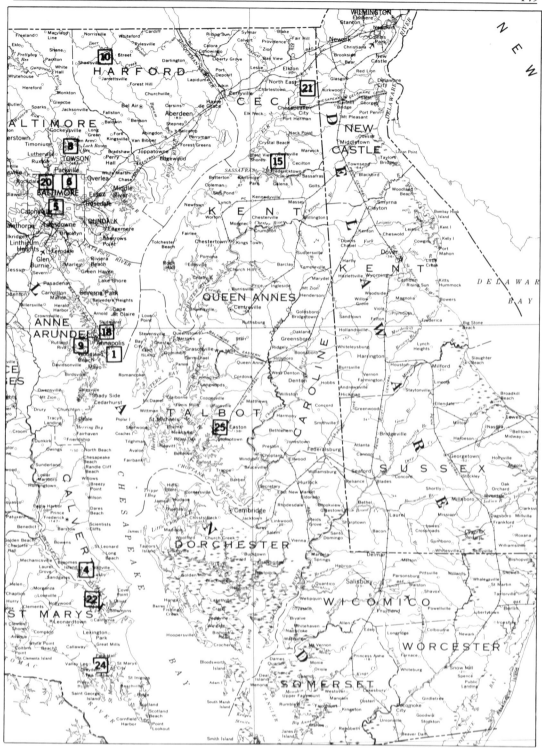

A group of individuals who are near in age and interest will agree fairly well on what they want to see. If all tolerate walking well, for example, garden visits are unlimited. However, for a group of mixed stamina or abilities, gardens with a variety of options for viewing and activities should be chosen. This will allow the fleet of foot room to move in while the individuals seeking a bench or two with scenic views can enjoy a less active visit. If a day of garden hopping is in the plan, the coordinator needs to contact the gardens involved and make any necessary arrangements.

Groups of school children may find several gardens interesting. Four gardens that are especially set up to receive children are Brookside, Carroll County Farm Museum and Gardens, National Colonial Farm, and St. Mary's City. Children may find Ladew Topiary Garden especially interesting. In all of these gardens there are differences in what is expected of children. Sensory programs for children usually allow and encourage children to pick, smell, and taste the plant material being seen. Other gardens are for looking not touching.

Groups with handicapped or elderly visitors need to be sure of the accessibility of restrooms, stopping spots for small rests within the garden under consideration, and adequate numbers of able visitors to assist the visitor in need. Lunch breaks might need to be longer and extra time planned for restroom stops. Best yet, if the garden has a small tour cart for the handicapped or elderly person, the garden staff needs to be notified in advance.

General Plans

Visitors wishing to take lunch with them will need to know about receptive spots for their noon repast. If the group is planning to utilize a tea room, reservations probably are necessary. If going by car into a congested area with one-way streets and difficult parking situations, drivers should know the directions in advance to avoid the hazards of trying to convoy. Parking change should be acquired ahead of time. Ticketing is strictly enforced in both Annapolis and Easton.

With plans well made and Mother Nature's cooperation, you can expect to see gardens year round. All of the gardens in this book have been open to sharing their beauties, their knowledge, and, in case of emergency, their assistance. The gardens include the beautiful, the instructive, those in memory, and those with special purpose.

The benefit of this small book is to reveal the public gardens and arboreta of the state of Maryland. We are blessed to have so many. They serve the many purposes we ask of them. They instruct us, amaze us, strike us with their beauty, cause us to laugh at the design of their stylist, and give us peace by their measurement of removal from the hustle and bustle of our work-world. We listen to the winds of the world in their treetops, hear bird song, and see a beauty in their flowers that we cannot create.

Not all of the gardens are beautiful; it is not their purpose. By looking at the thumbnail sketch of the gardens in this book, one can pick out those that match the visitor's expectations. Knowing what to expect upon arrival allows for greater success in making the trip.

These gardens are for all seasons. Not only are there seasons when each garden is at its company best, but also there are gardens that are beautiful for every month of the year. Visitor, go in expectation of beauty, peace, instruction, and pleasure and receive all that they have to give you. Enjoy.

A Checklist for Trips to Gardens

- Read information about the garden: type, hours, accessibility, fee, lunchrooms, facilities, location.
- Calculate distance/time for the total trip.
- Call ahead for the latest information.
- Make arrangements for groups and individuals needing assistance, or if you are coordinating more than one garden visit in one trip, call all gardens involved.
- Talk to children about what they are going to see, e.g. a garden looks a lot like a park without playground equipment. They will be more interested in plants with a little help.
- Visit a garden with real expectations of what the garden offers by reading the information on the garden rather than looking at the pictures which will be for promotion, rather than as an image of a perfect garden.
- Obtain information on bloom timing by calling as the season approaches. This can be important if you wish to see particular specimens or a single-season garden. The call will also alert the expectant visitor if bad weather has sent the garden to the sidelines for the season.
- Be aware before you go that in case of emergency, you should notify the nearest garden assistant who will most likely be able to assist you promptly. Gardens are part of their communities and information will be available on the nearest ambulance, Medevac helicopter, or hospital.
